INTRODUCTION TO

Brokerage Operations Department Procedures

Second Edition

NEW YORK INSTITUTE OF FINANCE

NEW YORK • TORONTO • SYDNEY • TOKYO • SINGAPORE

Library of Congress Cataloging-in-Publication Data

Introduction to brokerage operations department procedures.
Includes index.
ISBN 0-13-478975-X
1. Stockbrokers—United States. 2. Securities industry—United States. I. New York Institute of Finance.
HG4928.5.I57 1988   88-17846
332.6'2'068   CIP

A D'Maracra Product

Printed in the United States of America

10   9   8   7   6   5

This publication is designed to provide accurate and authoritative information in regard to the subject matter covered. It is sold with the understanding that the publisher is not engaged in rendering legal, accounting, or other professional service. If legal advice or other expert assistance is required, the services of a competent professional person should be sought.
—From the Declaration of Principles jointly adopted by a Committee of the American Bar Association and a Committee of Publishers and Associations

ISBN 0-13-478975-X

ATTENTION: CORPORATIONS AND SCHOOLS
NYIF books are available at quantity discounts with bulk purchase for educational, business, or sales promotional use. For information, please write to: New York Institute of Finance, Business Information and Publishing, 2 Broadway, New York, NY 10004-2283. Please supply: title of book, ISBN number, quantity, how the book will be used, date needed.

NEW YORK INSTITUTE OF FINANCE
2 Broadway
New York, N.Y. 10004-2283
(212) 859-5000
A Simon & Schuster Company

On the World Wide Web at http://www.phdirect.com

Prentice-Hall International (UK) Limited, *London*
Prentice-Hall of Australia Pty. Limited, *Sydney*
Prentice-Hall Canada Inc., *Toronto*
Prentice-Hall Hispanoamericana, S.A., *Mexico*
Prentice-Hall of India Private Limited, *New Delhi*
Prentice-Hall of Japan, Inc., *Tokyo*
Simon & Schuster Asia Pte. Ltd., *Singapore*
Editora Prentice-Hall do Brasil, Ltda., *Rio de Janeiro*

Contents

Introduction, xi

1

Forms of Business Organization, 1

THE PROPRIETORSHIP, 1
 Advantages of the Proprietorship, 2
 Disadvantages of the Proprietorship, 2
 The Problem of Raising Capital, 3
THE PARTNERSHIP, 3
 Disadvantages of the Partnership, 3
THE CORPORATION, 4
 Advantages of a Corporation, 4
 Management of the Corporation, 5

2

The Securities Industry, 7

KINDS OF SECURITIES HOUSES, 7
 The Member Firm, 8
 The Investment Banking Firm, 8
 The Over-the-Counter Firm, 8

THE DIFFERENCE BETWEEN A BROKER
   AND A DEALER, 9
THE UNDERWRITER, 10
MULTISERVICE FIRMS, 10
REGULATION OF THE SECURITIES INDUSTRY, 11
     Federal Laws, 11
     State Laws, 12

3

Stock, 13

TYPES OF STOCK, 13
COMMON STOCK, 14
     Rights of Common Stockholders, 15
     Par Value of Common Stock, 17
     Market Value of Common Stock, 17
PREFERRED STOCK, 18
     Par Value of Preferred Stock, 19
     Types of Preferred Stock, 19
DIVIDENDS, 23
RIGHTS AND WARRANTS, 24
     Rights, 24
     Warrants, 25
     The Certificate, 29

4

Corporate Bonds, 31

WHAT IS A BOND? 32
     Face Value, 32
     Maturity Date, 34
     Interest Rate, 34
     Purchase Price, 34
HOW BONDS DIFFER FROM STOCK, 35
TYPES OF CORPORATE BONDS, 36
     Bearer Bond, 36
     Registered Bond, 36
     Serial Bond, 36
     Callable Bond, 37
     Convertible Bond, 37
     Sinking Fund, 37

Secured Bonds, 37
Unsecured Bonds, 39
BANK-ISSUED DEBT SECURITIES, 39

5
Government and
Municipal Debt Securities, 41

U.S. TREASURY BILLS, NOTES, AND BONDS, 41
T Bills, 42
T Notes and T Bonds, 42
Settlement of U.S. Treasury Securities, 42
MORTGAGE-BACKED SECURITIES, 43
GNMAs, 43
Other Mortgage-Backed Securities, 43
Trading Mortgage-Backed Securities, 44
MUNICIPAL BONDS AND NOTES, 44
Trading Municipals, 44
Kinds of Municipal Bonds, 45
Municipal Notes, 45

6
Other Instruments, 47

MUTUAL FUNDS, 47
OPTIONS, 47
FUTURES CONTRACTS, 48

7
The Exchanges, 51

WHAT IS A STOCK EXCHANGE? 52
THE NEW YORK STOCK EXCHANGE, 53
The Administration of the NYSE, 53
Membership, 54
Requirements for Membership, 55
TYPES OF BROKERS, 56
Commission House Broker, 57
Two-Dollar Broker, 57
Registered Floor Trader, 57

Specialist, 58
Bond Broker, 59
ODD LOT TRANSACTIONS, 60
LISTING SECURITIES
   FOR TRADING ON THE NYSE, 61
TRADING ON THE NYSE, 61
THE AMERICAN STOCK EXCHANGE, 63
Administration, 63
Requirements for
   Membership in the Amex, 63
Trading on the Amex, 64

8

The Over-the-Counter Market, 65

THE NATURE OF THE OTC MARKET, 65
SECURITIES TRADED IN THE OTC MARKET, 67
BROKERS AND DEALERS, 67
OVER-THE-COUNTER FIRMS, 68
Investment Banking House, 68
Bond House, 69
Over-the-Counter Securities House, 69
Dealer's Broker (Broker's Broker), 69
REGULATION OF THE OTC MARKET, 70
MEMBERSHIP IN THE NASD, 70
TRADING IN THE OTC MARKET, 71
THE MARKET MAKERS, 72
The Bid and Asked, 72
Quotations in the OTC Market, 72
How a Trade Is Made in the OTC Market, 74
PUBLICIZING OTC QUOTATIONS, 75
Selected Quotations, 76
The Pink Sheets, 76

9

Operations: An Overview, 77

CUSTOMERS AND CUSTOMERS' ACCOUNTS, 78
OPENING AN ACCOUNT, 80
NEW ACCOUNTS, 81
Individual Cash Account, 81

Margin Account, 83
Joint Account, 83
Power-of-Attorney Account, 84
Corporate Account, 84
Other Accounts, 85

1 0
The Order Room, 87

CUSTOMERS' ORDERS, 87
THE ORDER FORM, 89
Contents of the Order Form, 89
KINDS OF ORDERS, 91
Market Orders, 91
Limit Orders, 92
Stop Orders, 93
Other Kinds of Orders, 94
SHORT SALES, 95
PROCESSING THE ORDER, 96
Exchange Systems, 96
Over-the-Counter Executions, 97
HOW ORDERS ARE EXECUTED, 98
Executing an Order on an Exchange, 98
Executing an Order on the OTC Market, 99

1 1
The Purchase and Sales Department, 101

RECORDING, 102
FIGURATION, 102
COMPARISON AND RECONCILEMENT, 108
How Executed Trades Are Compared, 109
Firm-to-Firm or Broker-to-Broker Comparison,
109
The Clearing House, 109
Work of the Clearing Corporation, 114
Netted Balance Orders, 116
Continuous Net Settlement, 118
Money Settlement, 119
Ex-Clearing Corporation Trades, 120
Reconcilement, 120
PREPARING THE CUSTOMER'S CONFIRMATION, 122

The Amount, 124
The Commission, 124
The Total, or Net, Amount, 125
The SEC Fee, 125
BOOKING, 125

12
The Margin Department, 127

HANDLING CASH ACCOUNTS, 128
HANDLING MARGIN ACCOUNTS, 130
The Margin Agreement, 131
Basic Terms Used in Margin Accounts, 131
REGULATION OF MARGIN ACCOUNTS, 137
Regulation T (Reg T), 137
Initial Margin Requirements, 137
Minimum Equity, 138
Time for Deposit of Margin, 138
Minimum Maintenance Requirements, 139
Restricted Accounts, 140
Special Memorandum Accounts (SMAs), 141
A CASE SUMMARY, 141
THE ROLES OF THE MARGIN DEPARTMENT, 145
Account Maintenance, 145
Sales Support, 145
Clearance for Issuance of Checks, 145
Items Due, 146
Extensions, 146
Close-Outs, 147
Delivery of Securities, 147

13
The Cashiers Department, 149

RECEIVE AND DELIVER, 150
The Settlement Cycle, 150
Functions of a Depository, 152
Institutional Customers, 155
Clearing Corporation:
Continuous Net Settlement, 155
Money Settlement, 157

Good Delivery, 157
The Settlement Process, 161
VAULTING, 162
Segregated (Seg) Securities, 163
HYPOTHECATION (BANK LOAN), 164
STOCK LOAN, 164
Repurchase Agreements (Repos), 165
THE SECURITY (STOCK) TRANSFER, 165
Steps in the Transfer of Stock, 166
Duties of the Transfer Section, 167
Transfer through the
Depository Trust Company, 171
REORGANIZATIONS, TENDERS, AND
SPIN-OFFS, 171

14
The Stock Record Department, 173
HOW THE STOCK RECORD IS KEPT, 174
Long (Debit) Position, 175
Short (Credit) Position, 177
DAILY STOCK RECORD, 177
WEEKLY (MAIN) STOCK RECORD, 179
THE AUDIT, 180

15
Cash Accounting, 183
CREDITS AND DEBITS, 183
DAILY ACTIVITY, 186
CLOSING THE BOOKS, 187

16
The Dividend Department, 189
CASH DIVIDENDS, 190
STOCK DIVIDENDS, 191
STOCK SPLITS, 192
THE ROLE OF THE DIVIDEND DEPARTMENT, 193
Dividend Rate, 194
Declaration Date, 195

Payable Date, 195
Record Date, 195
Ex-Dividend Date, 196
DEPOSITORIES, 197
CLAIMING DIVIDENDS FOR CUSTOMERS, 197
BOND INTEREST, 200

1 7

The Proxy Department, 201

STOCKHOLDER VOTE BY PROXY, 202
THE PROXY, 202
THE RECORD DATE, 204
HOW THE PROXY DEPARTMENT
   HELPS CORPORATIONS, 205

Glossary, 207

Index, 237

Introduction

Our purpose in writing this book is to explain, in simple form, that most complicated area known as the brokerage industry's operations function.

A firm base is first established. Early chapters are devoted to an explanation of corporate structure, an overview of the securities industry, the difference between listed and unlisted trading, and the basic types of equity and debt securities. Only then do we begin to paint in the picture of the many departments involved when a customer's order is entered and executed.

The operations division plays an important role in the securities industry. The failure of this division to perform its functions properly can cause a breakdown in the services that a securities house renders to its customers. It can also mean a loss of many thousands of dollars to the securities house.

The several departments that make up the operations division are interrelated. A breakdown in the work of any division means a breakdown all along the line. Thus, to perform your job better, you must know how it fits in with the work of the other divisions.

The sequence is logical and, as closely as is practicable, follows an order for securities from its inception through to its final payment and delivery. Although this work has been designed as a primer for the newer brokerage firm employee, we are confident that it will also be valuable to *anyone* who wishes to learn about this fascinating aspect of the brokerage business.

Readers should find the glossary at the end of this book to be especially helpful.

The securities industry is a *service* industry. The success of any securities house depends on the speed and accuracy with which it services its customers. Many factors influence the customer in selecting the securities house with which he places his orders. Among these are the following:

- How quickly is his order executed?
- How quickly does he receive his securities if he is purchasing?
- How quickly does he receive his money if he is selling?
- Is the transaction handled accurately?

An error anywhere along the way means that the error will be carried through the steps that follow. And a customer may take his business elsewhere because of an error. Even if he does not, an error can still be costly in terms of the time and effort needed to correct it.

To Illustrate: A customer places an order with a firm to buy 100 shares of stock. An error is made in handling the transaction. Let us take a look at just one of the many possible consequences of that error.

Instead of executing the order to buy 100 shares, the order goes through to buy 10 shares. Result: A new order to buy 100 shares must be entered and executed. Meanwhile, your firm owns 10 shares of stock that it doesn't want and that it now has to sell. If the price of the stock has gone up, then the customer may demand the difference between the price at which the 100 shares should have been bought and the price at which it was bought. The firm will most likely credit the customer's account for this difference. Although the firm may make a small profit on the sale of the 10 shares, it will not be enough to make up for the credit to the customer's account. In addition, there is the dollars-and-cents cost involved in making the necessary corrections. This cost can wipe out the commission on the trade.

As you can see, the brokerage firm's operation can be successful only if *everyone* performs his or her assignments diligently. Through everyone's conscientious participation, a firm can continue to earn a profit and remain in business. The focal point for everyone's effort must remain always on the customers, their orders for purchases or sales, and their security accounts.

One last note: In the many years since the first edition of this book was published, the back office of a securities firm has changed drastically. With record volumes in the stock and other markets, the typical operations division has become all but fully automated. In practice, many of the functions described in this book, therefore, are performed by computers.

Automation may relieve the operations staff of workload, but not of the need to know their individual responsibilities and how to meet them. So the descriptions of various operations departments' tasks are therefore manual in context. This is for the sake of your understanding the steps and procedures behind the computerized functions.

1   Forms
of Business
Organization

There are three basic forms of business organization—the proprietorship, the partnership, and the corporation. The most important for our purposes is the corporation. Only the corporation issues securities that are traded (bought and sold) publicly. Before discussing the corporation, let us examine the other two forms of business organization.

THE PROPRIETORSHIP

The proprietorship is the earliest known form of business organization; it is also the simplest.

A *proprietorship* is a business owned by only one person, who is called the *proprietor,* or owner. Many small businesses—such as a shoe repair shop or a neighborhood dry cleaner—have only one owner. Such businesses are usually operated as proprietorships.

Advantages of the Proprietorship

A person who wants to do business as a proprietorship does not have to have legal papers drawn up. Nor does he usually have to pay any organization fees. However, he may have to pay a license tax to begin business.

As a proprietor, the owner has sole control over the operation and management of the business. And if the business is successful, all the profits belong to the owner.

Disadvantages of the Proprietorship

On the other hand, if the business loses money and goes into debt, the owner is responsible for the payment of these debts. This responsibility is called the *owner's liability.* And in a proprietorship, the owner's liability is unlimited.

To illustrate: Mary Jones gets together $5,000 and opens a small retail store. However, the business loses money and is finally $9,000 in debt. Because the business is a proprietorship, Jones has unlimited liability for the debts of the business. In other words, she has to pay the entire $9,000 debt. Jones must pay, even if it means selling her home, her car, and other property. What is more, she has to pay the whole debt, even though she invested only $5,000 in the business to begin with.

A proprietorship is so much a one-person business that the proprietor *is* the business. If the proprietor dies or leaves the business, the business will end. And although a new proprietor may take over after the former owner dies or leaves the business, the business does not legally continue. A new owner creates a new proprietorship.

The Problem of Raising Capital

Last, there's the question of raising *capital*—that is, money used to start the business and to keep it going. Businesses use capital for such things as to pay rent on space in which to operate, to hire workers and pay their salaries, and to buy supplies. Some types of business organizations find it easier to raise capital than others. As business organizations go, the proprietorship probably is least able to raise capital. In a proprietorship, the capital is usually limited to that which the owner can provide, plus what the owner can borrow on personal credit.

THE PARTNERSHIP

Two or more persons who carry on a business as co-owners are called *partners*. The business they own is called a *partnership*. There are several kinds of partnerships. However, here we shall talk about only the general partnership—the most common form of partnership.

Disadvantages of the Partnership

Like the proprietorship, the partnership form of business organization has certain disadvantages. For example, each partner is jointly and severally responsible along with the other partners for the debts of the partnership.

To illustrate: Adams and Bacon form a partnership. The partnership incurs debts of $10,000. Adams and Bacon are each individually responsible for payment of these debts. If the business does not have the $10,000, Adams and Bacon themselves must pay the debts. They may be forced to sell their homes, automobiles, and other property to raise money to do so.

A partnership also has a limited life. Thus, a partnership usually ends on the death or withdrawal of one of the partners. It also ends if the agreement between the partners ends and is not renewed.

Because of its limited life, it is difficult for a partnership to raise capital. Normally, the capital of a partnership is limited to the amount that the partners can contribute or that they can borrow.

THE CORPORATION

As we have seen, the proprietorship and its owner are one and the same. The general partnership and its partners are also one and the same. Thus, if you want to sue a proprietorship, you sue the owner. And if you want to sue a general partnership, you bring your action against the partners. If you want to sue a corporation, however, you bring your action against the corporation.

A *corporation* is separate and distinct from its owners, who are called *stockholders* or *shareholders*. In other words, a corporation is an artificial being, or entity, created under the laws of a state. Under the law, a corporation is a person. It can sue and be sued. It pays income taxes. Its existence continues, despite changes of ownership.

Advantages of a Corporation

The legal entity (being) concept gives the corporation many advantages not enjoyed by the proprietorship or the partnership. One advantage is that a corporation may enjoy a continuous existence: If one or even all the owners sell their shares, it will not end the corporation's life; the corporation will still continue to exist.

Another advantage is that the stockholders in a corporation have a limited liability. This liability is usually limited to the amount of a stockholder's investment in the corporation.

To illustrate: An investor can place $5,000 in the common stock of a corporation. Later, the corporation goes bankrupt. All the investor may lose is $5,000, and usually that is all he will lose. The corporation may have debts of thousands, even millions, of dollars. However, as a stockholder, you will not be responsible for paying these debts.

A major advantage in doing business as a corporation is the ability to raise large amounts of capital. This the corporation can do either through the sale of stock (ownership interests) or of bonds (debt securities), or both. The people who buy these stocks and bonds can then sell them either on a stock exchange or in the over-the-counter market. (We discuss this in more detail in later chapters.)

Management of the Corporation

The stockholders of a corporation do not themselves manage the business of the corporation. Instead, these shareholders elect directors who set policy. The directors, in turn, appoint officers (a president, treasurer, secretary) who run the business in line with the policies set by the directors.

2   The
Securities Industry

The securities industry consists of the stock, options, and futures exchanges, the over-the-counter market, and the brokers and dealers who trade on these markets. It has played a very important role in the growth of American business. By providing a market for the purchase and sale of stocks and bonds, the industry has made investment in these securities more attractive to the public.

Let us take a look at the securities houses (broker and dealer firms) and their functions. Most securities houses are organized as partnerships or corporations. Some do business as proprietorships.

KINDS OF SECURITIES HOUSES

Securities houses are generally classified according to the kind of business they do.

The Member Firm

The member firm, also called a brokerage firm, gets its name from the fact that it is a member of an organized stock exchange—for example, the New York Stock Exchange or the American Stock Exchange, or the Chicago Board Option Exchange. The basic business of a member firm is to buy and sell securities for its customers on the stock exchange of which it is a member.

The Investment Banking Firm

The business of an investment banking firm is to distribute new securities to the public. It does this by buying issues from the corporation, and then selling these securities to the public at a price that includes the firm's profit. Another name for the investment banking firm is *underwriter*. When an investment banker forms a group of brokerage firms that will distribute, or underwrite, a new issue, that group is known as a *syndicate*.

The Over-the-Counter (OTC) Firm

The OTC firm does *not* buy and sell securities on an exchange. Instead, it buys and sells securities *over the counter*. The purchase and sale of securities in a place other than on an exchange is known as *over-the-counter trading*. And firms that do this kind of trading are known as *over-the-counter firms*.

Many securities houses do business in all three areas. Thus, the same firm may execute orders for customers on an exchange or in the over-the-counter market. The firm may also act as an underwriter for newly issued securities.

THE DIFFERENCE BETWEEN
A BROKER AND A DEALER

A *broker* is an agent; he buys and sells for the account of his customers. The broker's compensation is the commission that is paid to him by the customer for his (the broker's) services. For example, let us assume that you want to sell your home. You can go to a real estate broker and ask him to find a buyer. If he is successful, you pay him a commission for his services.

The same is true when you place an order with a broker to buy or sell a security. You are hiring the broker to act as your *agent*. When the trade is executed, he will charge you a commission for his services.

A member firm usually acts as a broker. The commission a member firm charges for executing an order is based on the quantity of shares or dollar amount of the transaction. The customer pays a commission when he buys a security and again when he sells it.

A *dealer,* on the other hand, buys and sells securities for his own account. He then tries to sell the securities to others at a higher price than he paid when he bought them. Because of this, we say that a dealer acts as a *principal.* Such dealers are also known as *market makers.* (See also Chapter 5.)

The dealer does not charge his customers a commission. Instead, he takes a *markup.* This markup is the difference between the price the dealer has paid for the security and the price he sells it for. Generally, the markup will not be more than 5% of the price the dealer paid for the security—often it will be less.

To Illustrate: You want to buy 100 shares of XYZ common stock. The stock is traded in the over-the-counter market. You could go to an over-the-counter firm and give the firm your order. The firm is able to buy the stock at $41 a share, or a total of $4,100 for the 100 shares. The firm might then sell the stock to you for $42 a share, or a total of $4,200. The difference between the price the firm paid for the stock ($4,100) and the price it sold the stock to you for ($4,200) is the markup. In this example, the markup is $100, that is, $4,200 minus $4,100.

Many member firms also trade in the OTC market. Some of these firms may execute orders in the OTC market as a broker. When they do, they will *not* take a markup; instead, they will charge their customers a commission for their services. This commission is often the same as that which the member firm would charge for executing the order on an exchange.

THE UNDERWRITER

You have already learned that the function of an investment banking firm—the underwriter—is to sell newly issued securities to the public. In other words, the investment banking firm helps corporations raise capital needed for the expansion of their plants and for other purposes.

In performing this function, the underwriter may act either on a *firm commitment* basis or on a *best efforts* basis. When acting on a firm commitment basis, the underwriter is acting as a dealer. That is, the underwriter has agreed to buy the entire issue from the corporation, at a specified price, in the hope that it can sell the securities to the public at a higher price, or markup.

When the underwriter agrees to sell the securities on a *best efforts* basis, it is also acting as a dealer. Here, however, the underwriter is not committed to buy the entire issue from the corporation. Instead, it has merely agreed to use its best efforts to sell the securities. In other words, the underwriter has to buy from the corporation only those securities it is able to sell.

MULTISERVICE FIRMS

Some firms are not restricted to a particular facet of the industry. These firms are known as *multiservice* organizations. They may offer their customers brokerage facilities for listing trading, principal positioning for OTC customer trades, and syndicate participation. The firm's expertise and product mix will determine which service or services they will offer to their customer base.

REGULATION OF THE SECURITIES INDUSTRY

Member firms are subject to—and base many of their procedures on—the rules and regulations of the federal and state agencies, of the exchanges, and of various self-regulatory organizations *(SROs)*. Some of these many directives govern firm-to-firm dealings; others affect customer-to-firm relationships. Yet rarely are customers aware of all the rules and regulations that affect them. The brokerage firms must therefore act as "watchdogs" for their clients, maintaining their accounts in accordance with all applicable rules if they are to conduct a violation-free business.

Federal Laws

Federal laws regulate the sale of securities and the conduct of business in the securities market. The federal laws are administered by the Securities and Exchange Commission (SEC), the Federal Reserve Board (The "Fed"), and the Commodities Futures Trading Commission (CFTC) (which regulates the trading of commodities futures on the futures exchanges). (Commodities futures and the futures exchanges are discussed in a later chapter.) The Fed regulates margin lending; its rules fix the maximum amount of credit a securities house may give to its customers for the purchase of securities.

The SEC regulates all other activities. For example:

1. Before a corporation can first offer its securities for sale to the public—either directly or through an

underwriter—the corporation must give the SEC detailed information in the form of a Registration Statement.

2 . A stock exchange cannot do business unless it is registered with the SEC. Registration means supplying the SEC with detailed information about the exchange's rules and procedures and about its ability to supervise the activities of its members.

3 . Before it can do business in the OTC market, a securities house must register with the SEC as well as with the NASD to be a broker-dealer. Here, registration means filing detailed information with the SEC, including the background of the firm's partners or stockholders, their education and experience, and financial status. The registration must be approved by the SEC. Thereafter, if the firm commits any infraction of the rules, the SEC may suspend or revoke its registration.

State Laws

State securities laws—more commonly known as *blue sky laws*—also regulate the sale of securities and the ways in which the securities houses conduct their business in any particular state. Most blue sky laws are similar to the federal laws. However, blue sky laws are generally stricter.

The federal laws provide for disclosure of relevant information. State blue sky laws, on the other hand, are *permit,* or *licensing,* laws. The state administrators have broad authority to deny registration for a wide variety of reasons.

In our ever-changing industry, new or variations of existing products are constantly being brought to market. Each variation is intended to fill a need or niche in the marketplace, to better serve some investor's need. The following chapters present the more popular of these issues.

3   Stock

Stocks and bonds are the most common kinds of securities that a corporation issues. A corporation can issue two kinds of stock—common and preferred—and several kinds of bonds. In this chapter you will learn about those securities known as *stock*.

TYPES OF STOCK

Common stock represents the voting ownership of a corporation and is perpetual with the life of the corporation. The securities are denominated in *shares,* with 100 shares comprising a *round lot* unit for trading purposes. Between 1 share and 99 shares is known as an *odd lot.*

The common stockholders vote for the board of directors of the corporation. The board, in turn, manages the company. Common stockholders are also called upon to vote on critical issues facing the company.

Some, but not all corporations, pay dividends to their common shareholders. The dividends must be declared by the board of directors and are paid on a per-share basis.

Preferred stock is another form of ownership. This security is also issued in shares, with 100 shares comprising a trading round lot. On some stock exchanges, due to their high price, certain preferreds trade in 10-share round lots. Unlike common stock, preferred stocks do not give owners the right to vote. Preferred stocks are supposed to pay a stipulated rate of dividend. Dividends are usually paid on a quarterly basis, and they must be paid before common stockholders may receive dividends.

COMMON STOCK

At the time a corporation is organized, it issues shares of common stock. Figure 3–1 is a specimen certificate of common stock.

Each share of common stock represents an ownership interest of the shareholder in the corporation. The greater the number of shares a shareholder owns, the greater is his ownership interest in the corporation.

To illustrate: A corporation has 1,000 shares of common stock outstanding, and one person owns 100 shares of this stock. This person then has a 10% ownership interest in the corporation (100 shares divided by 1,000 shares).

Sometimes a corporation will issue different kinds of common stock—Class A common stock and Class B common stock. These two classes of stock may differ in several ways. One class of stock may have the right to vote for the election of directors, whereas the other class may be denied that right. Or, when the company pays a dividend (distributes its earnings) to its stockholders, one class of stock may receive a larger share of the dividend than the other class of stock. Also, if the company is liquidated (goes out of business), one class of stock may receive a greater share of the assets than the other class of stock.

Rights of Common Stockholders

Ownership of *common stock* normally carries with it certain rights or privileges. Among these are the following:

1. The right to vote for the election of the board of directors. The directors are responsible for managing the corporation.

2. The right to receive dividends when they are declared by the directors. Dividends are a distribution to stockholders of the corporation's earnings. The common stockholders are not entitled to dividends unless declared by the directors. *Cash dividends* are paid on a per-share basis. *Stock dividends* are paid as a percentage of the shares owned.

3. The right to transfer ownership of the shares. This right may be exercised by selling the shares, or by making a gift of the shares, or by bequeathing them to someone in a will.

4. The right to vote on questions affecting the corporation as a whole. For example, the shareholders could vote on whether the corporation should sell its assets. Assets means everything the corporation owns—land, buildings, machinery, and so on.

5. The right to inspect the corporate books. For example, a shareholder can examine the stock register or the list of stockholders.

6. The right to share in money obtained by the dissolution of the corporation. However, first the corporation's creditors and other persons having a preference must be paid. *Dissolution* means the termination of the corporation's existence.

Figure 3–1. A Certificate of Common Stock

000-2271-68

Par Value of Common Stock

Most corporations assign a *par value* to each share of stock. This is printed on the stock certificate as shown in Figure 3–1.

The par value has no relation to the *market price,* or *market value,* of the stock. Its only importance is at the time the stock is first issued. Then the par value represents the minimum, or lowest, price the company must receive for each share of stock that it sells.

To illustrate: A company assigns a *par value* of, say, $10 to each share of common stock. This means that the company must receive at least $10 in cash or property for each share that it sells. But it may get more. If the company has issued 1,000 shares of common stock, it should receive at least $10,000. This money becomes the original capital of the corporation.

If a company wishes, it may issue *no par value* stock. The advantage of this kind of stock is that the company can sell the shares for whatever it believes these shares will bring in the market.

Market Value of Common Stock

Once stock has been sold to the public, its price is determined by the value investors place on it. This value is called the *market price,* or *market value.* It will usually depend on what investors believe this value should be. In arriving at their decision, the investors will consider such factors as the earnings for each share of stock, the company's dividend policy, and the company's future prospects (how well the company is expected to do).

The par value of a stock has no effect on its market price. In fact, the market price of a stock is not fixed by the corporation. Nor is it fixed by anyone else. Instead, the market price of a stock is determined by the lowest price a seller is willing to sell it for, and the highest price a buyer is willing to pay for it.

PREFERRED STOCK

Preferred stock also represents an ownership interest in a corporation. It is called *preferred* stock because of preferences given to the holders of this stock over the holders of common stock. Figures 3–2a and 3–2b show a preferred stock certificate.

Generally, the preferred stockholder has the right to receive dividends before any dividend is declared, or paid, on the common stock. The dividend is printed on the stock certificate. It is shown as a definite dollar amount for each share or as a fixed percentage of the par value of the stock.

Also, the preferred stockholder usually has a prior claim against the assets of the company in the event of its dissolution. For example, if the company has to liquidate its assets, the preferred stockholder usually will be paid the value of his shares before any payment is made to the common stockholders.

However, unlike the common stockholder, the holder of preferred stock usually may not be entitled to vote for the election of the board of directors. Thus, because the preferred stockholder may have no voting rights and because his right to dividends may be limited to a fixed amount, we say that the preferred stockholder has *limited ownership rights* in the corporation.

There are two types of preferred stock dividends: dollar preferred and percent preferred.

- *Dollar preferred:* For example, Dahl $8 preferred stock is to pay $8 per share per year.

- *Percent preferred:* A percent preferred pays its dividend based on a percentage of the preferred's par value. Therefore, if a Dahl 8% preferred has a par value of $100, it is supposed to pay $8 per share per year. On the other hand, if the preferred has a par value of $50, the preferred will pay $4 per share per year. (Par value is the method used for converting shares into dollars on the corporation's balance sheet. It has nothing to do with the market value or book value.)

Par Value of Preferred Stock

Like common stock, the preferred stock may be either par value or *no par value* stock. Here, again, this has no relation to its *market value.* However, if the preferred stock has a par value, then the dividend—which may be either a fixed percentage or definite dollar amount—will be based on that par value.

To illustrate: A "$100 par value, $4\frac{1}{2}$% preferred" would pay a fixed amount of $4.50 per share ($100 x $4\frac{1}{2}$%). But a "$50 par value, 5% preferred" would pay $2.50 per share ($50 x 5%).

If the preferred stock has *no par value,* however, the dividend will simply be stated as "$5 per share" or "$2.50 per share" or such other dollar amount per share as the issuing corporation may have assigned.

Types of Preferred Stock

Normally, a corporation will issue only one class of common stock, but it may issue more than one class, or kind, of preferred stock. The kind of preferred that a stock is will be shown on the stock certificate.

If a corporation issues more than one series of preferred stock, it may designate one as *first preferred* and the other as *second preferred.* Or it may call one *prior preferred* and the other simply *preferred.*

This establishes the priority of one class over the other as to dividends or distribution of assets, or both. For example, the holder of *first preferred* stock will be entitled to receive his dividend before any dividend is paid to the holder of *second preferred* stock.

Again, a company may classify preferred stock by its dividend preferences. For example, *participating* or *nonparticipating, cumulative* or *noncumulative.* These terms are explained in the following paragraphs.

Figure 3–2a. A Preferred Stock Certificate (front)

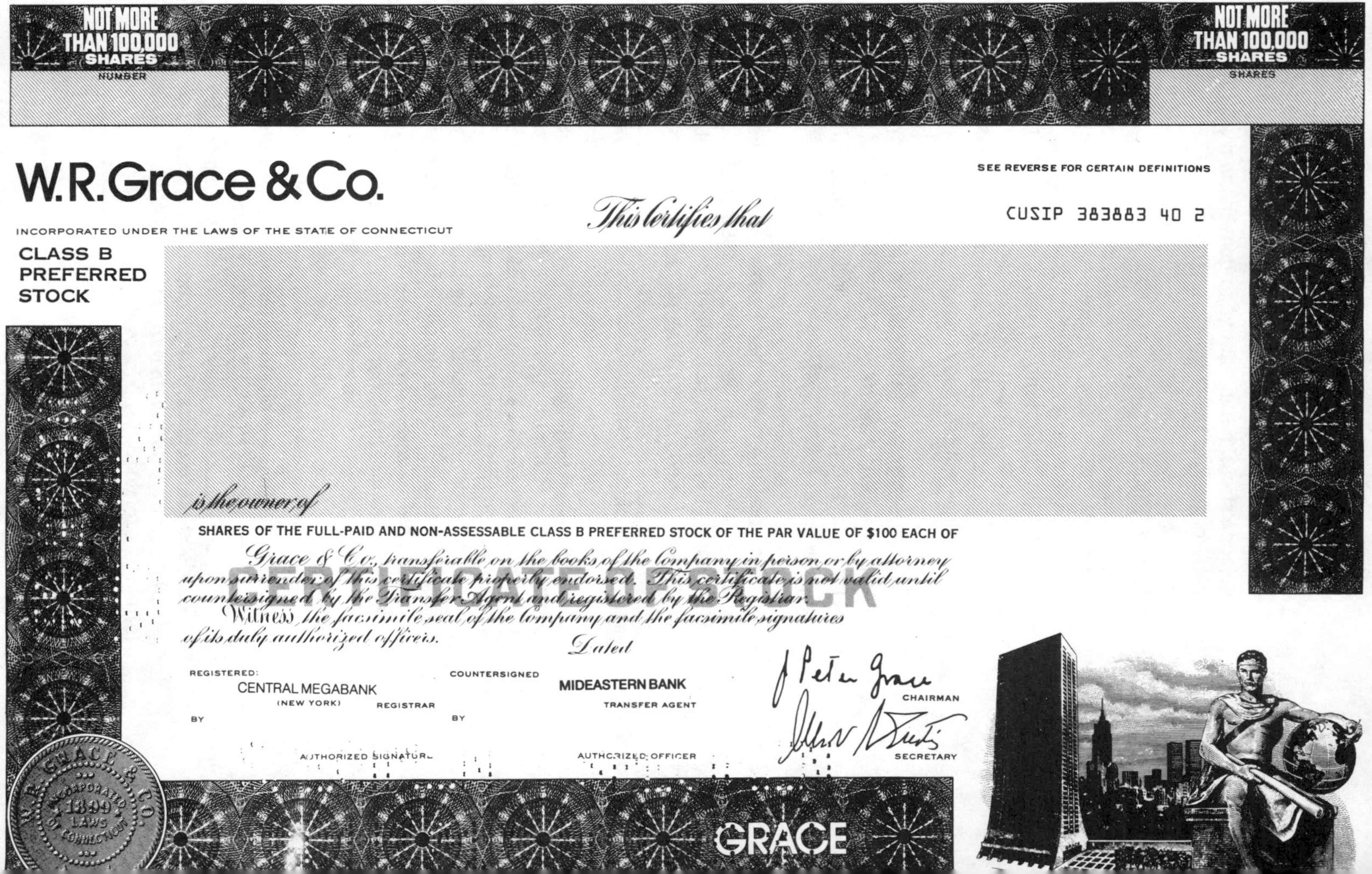

RN 570:39

NOT MORE THAN 100,000 SHARES

NUMBER

NOT MORE THAN 100,000 SHARES

SHARES

W.R. Grace & Co.

INCORPORATED UNDER THE LAWS OF THE STATE OF CONNECTICUT

CLASS B PREFERRED STOCK

SEE REVERSE FOR CERTAIN DEFINITIONS

This Certifies that

CUSIP 383883 40 2

is the owner of

SHARES OF THE FULL-PAID AND NON-ASSESSABLE CLASS B PREFERRED STOCK OF THE PAR VALUE OF $100 EACH OF

Grace & Co., transferable on the books of the Company in person or by attorney upon surrender of this certificate properly endorsed. This certificate is not valid until countersigned by the Transfer Agent and registered by the Registrar.

Witness the facsimile seal of the Company and the facsimile signatures of its duly authorized officers.

CERTIFICATE OF STOCK

Dated

REGISTERED:
CENTRAL MEGABANK
(NEW YORK) REGISTRAR

BY

AUTHORIZED SIGNATURE

COUNTERSIGNED
MIDEASTERN BANK
TRANSFER AGENT

BY

AUTHORIZED OFFICER

J Peter Grace
CHAIRMAN

SECRETARY

W. R. GRACE & CO. INCORPORATED 1899 LAWS CONNECTICUT

GRACE

Figure 3–2b. A Preferred Stock Certificate (back)

A statement of the designations, terms, limitations and relative rights and preferences of the shares of each class authorized to be issued, any variations in relative rights and preferences between the shares of any series of any class so far as said rights and preferences shall have been fixed and determined and the authority or the Board of Directors of the Company to fix and determine any relative rights and preferences of any subsequent series will be furnished to the holder hereof without charge, upon request to the Secretary of the Company or to the Transfer Agent named on the face hereof.

The following abbreviations, when used in the inscription of ownership on the face of this certificate, shall be construed as though they were written out in full according to applicable laws or regulations.

JT TEN — As joint tenants, with right of survivorship, and not as tenants in common

TEN IN COM—As tenants in common

TEN BY ENT—As tenants by the entireties

Abbreviations in addition to those appearing above may be used.

For value received,_____ hereby sell, assign and transfer unto

_____

(PLEASE PRINT OR TYPEWRITE NAME AND ADDRESS OF ASSIGNEE)

_____

_____

_____ shares

of the capital stock represented by the within Certificate, and do hereby irrevocably constitute and appoint

_____ Attorney

to transfer the said stock on the books of the within named Company with full power of substitution in the premises.

Dated _____

Notice: The signature to this assignment must correspond with the name as written upon the face of the certificate in every particular, without alteration or enlargement or any change whatever.

Nonparticipating Preferred. Ordinarily, a preferred stockholder is not entitled to receive any dividends beyond the fixed or stipulated rates. Thus, an investor who owns "$100 par value, 5% preferred" is entitled to receive dividends of $5 a share before any dividends are distributed to the common stockholders. But he is not entitled to receive more than the $5 a share. Such preferred stock is called *nonparticipating* preferred.

Participating Preferred. To attract investors, a corporation may sometimes issue *participating* preferred stock. This means that the preferred stockholder, in addition to receiving his stipulated dividend, is given the right to participate with the common stockholder in any distributions of earnings. Participation may be made in any number of different ways.

To illustrate: One company has this arrangement: Preferred, $5 per share; then common stock, $5 per share; then preferred and common to share equally up to $1 per share in any one year.

Another company uses this arrangement: Preferred, $1.50 a share; then common, $1.50 a share; then preferred and common to share equally in the remainder.

Cumulative and Noncumulative Preferred. Dividends on preferred stock may also be *cumulative* or *noncumulative*. A *cumulative* dividend means that if the dividend on the preferred stock is not declared in a particular year, the dividend will accumulate or add up. This accumulation must be paid before any dividends can be declared on the common stock.

To illustrate: A corporation has outstanding "$4 cumulative preferred" stock. The earnings in a particular year are low. Because of this, the directors of the corporation decide to *pass,* or omit, payment of the dividend. This dividend of $4 a share will accumulate. The next year it must be paid, together with that year's dividend of $4 a share, before any dividends can be paid on the common stock.

On the other hand, if the dividend is *noncumulative,* and the corporation has omitted the dividend in a particular year, the dividend need not be made up before a dividend may be paid on the common stock.

Convertible Preferred. Still another type of preferred stock is the *convertible* preferred. Here, the holder receives the right to exchange the preferred stock for another security, usually a share or shares of common stock of the same company. The formula for making the exchange of convertible preferred stock for common stock is fixed by the company at the time the convertible preferred is issued.

DIVIDENDS

Throughout the discussion of common and preferred stock, we have spoken about the distribution of dividends to the holders of a corporation's stocks. Now, let's see in what forms dividends may be distributed.

Dividends are a distribution of the corporation's earnings to the stockholders in proportion to their stockholdings. Dividends are stated on an annual (yearly) basis, although payment is usually made quarterly (every three months). Thus, when we say a company pays a dividend of 20 cents a share we mean that the dividend is 20 cents a share each year. Generally, stockholders are not entitled to dividends unless dividends are declared by the corporation.

A corporation may declare that a dividend shall be paid in cash, in stock, or in property. Most companies pay *cash* dividends. These are expressed at so much per share—for instance, 50 cents a share or $1 a share.

Sometimes, in order to conserve its cash, a corporation may declare a *stock* dividend. This means that the dividend is paid in the company's own stock.

A corporation may be in the process of dissolution. That is, the corporation is terminating its existence. When that happens, the corporation may declare a dividend payable in corporate property. This kind of dividend is called a *property,* or *liquidating,* dividend.

RIGHTS AND WARRANTS

A company also may raise additional capital by issuing *rights* and *warrants* to current stockholders (see Figures 3–3a and 3–3b). Rights and warrants are similar in that both permit their holders to subscribe to the new shares. They differ in that rights are generally short-term, whereas warrants have much longer lives. Also, a corporation may have several warrant issues outstanding at one time, but it may offer only one rights issue at a time.

Rights

A *right,* or *subscription right,* is a privilege granted by a corporation to its stockholders to purchase new securities in proportion to the number of shares they own. Usually, rightholders are entitled to a purchase, or *subscription,* price that is lower than the stock's current market price. Rights are usually short-term in duration.

Generally, when a corporation decides to sell additional shares in an issue of securities, it will give those persons who already own stock in the company the right or opportunity to purchase additional shares of stock in proportion to their present holdings. For example, the corporation may give its stockholders the privilege of buying *one* new share of stock for each *ten* shares they now own.

Each stockholder entitled to this privilege receives a *right certificate* showing the exact number of rights to which he is entitled (see Figure 3–4). The rights must be exercised (exchanged for the stock) within a fixed period of time and at a stipulated price. The value of the right is considered part of the stock owner's capital. If the right is discarded, the owner loses money. Some investors who are not aware of this value treat rights as junk mail and throw them away. They are throwing away money.

Rights are issued when the corporation's charter contains a "preemptive rights" clause. The purpose of this clause is to protect stockholders from having their percentage ownership in the corporation diluted through the issuance of additional shares of their class of stock. By permitting the existing stockholders to subscribe to the new shares in proportion to what they currently own, the rights enable shareholders to maintain their percentage ownership. If the existing shareholders do not want to participate in the subscription, they may sell their rights or let them expire.

The rights usually give the stockholder the privilege of purchasing the stock at a price that is lower than the current market price. For example, if the market price of the stock is $54, the company might give its stockholders the privilege of buying the new stock at $45 a share. Because of this, *rights have a market value of their own* and can be sold.

If a stockholder wants to exercise his rights, he fills in the certificate and sends it to the corporation. He also sends a check or money order for the price of the additional shares he wants to buy. Or, if he wishes, a stockholder may sell his rights in the market at their prevailing market price. Whichever a stockholder decides to do must be done by the date stated in the rights certificate. After that date, the rights become worthless; that is, they can neither be exercised nor sold.

Warrants

A *warrant,* attached to another security, entitles the holder to convert the security into common stock or some other instrument at a set price during a specified period. The price set in the warrant is higher than the current market value of the common stock. Warrants are longer-term issues than rights.

Figure 3-3a. A Warrant (front)

WARRANT

THIS WARRANT WILL BE VOID IF NOT EXERCISED ON OR PRIOR TO MARCH 15, 1981

No. W

McCARRY CORPORATION

COMMON STOCK PURCHASE WARRANT

FOR THE PURCHASE OF

_____ SHARES

THIS CERTIFIES that, for value received, _____ Corporation, a Delaware corporation (hereinafter called the "Company"), upon the surrender of this Warrant, as hereinafter provided, to the Company at the corporate trust office in the City of New York of the Warrant Agent hereinafter mentioned (or of its successor as Warrant Agent), provided, and only if, this Warrant shall be so surrendered on or before March 15, 1981, will sell and deliver, or cause to be sold and delivered, to

or assigns, the number of fully paid and non-assessable shares set forth above of the Company's Common Stock, par value fifty cents per share, as constituted on the date of the Warrant Agreement hereinbelow mentioned, upon payment of the warrant price for the number of shares in respect of which this Warrant is exercised; provided, however, that under certain conditions set forth in said Warrant Agreement the number of shares of the Company's Common Stock purchasable upon the exercise of this Warrant may be increased or reduced and the warrant price may be adjusted, or securities other than shares of said Common Stock may become purchasable in lieu thereof upon the exercise of this Warrant. Subject to adjustment as aforesaid, the warrant price shall be $20 per share to and including March 15, 1976 and $22.50 from March 16, 1976 to and including March 15, 1981 (herein called the "warrant price"). As provided in said Warrant Agreement, the warrant price is payable, upon the exercise of this Warrant, either in cash or by certified check or bank draft payable in New York funds. No adjustment shall be made for any dividends on any shares of stock issuable upon exercise of this Warrant. The right of purchase represented by this Warrant is exercisable, at the election of the registered holder hereof, or his assigns, either in its entirety or from time to time for part only of the shares specified herein and, in the event that this Warrant is exercised in respect of less than all of such shares, a new Warrant for the remaining number of such shares will be issued on such surrender in accordance with instructions set forth in the election to purchase the form of which is printed on the reverse hereof.

Upon the exercise of this Warrant the form of election to purchase on the reverse hereof must be duly executed by the registered holder hereof, or his assigns, and the accompanying instructions for the registration and delivery of stock must be filled in.

This Warrant is issued under and the rights represented hereby are subject to the terms and provisions contained in a Warrant Agreement dated as of March 15, 1966, between the Company and CHEMICAL BANK NEW YORK TRUST COMPANY, as Warrant Agent, to all the terms and provisions of which the holder of this Warrant, by acceptance hereof, assents. Reference is hereby made to said Warrant Agreement for a more complete statement of the rights and limitations of rights of the registered holder hereof and his assigns, the rights and duties of the Warrant Agent and the rights and obligations of the Company thereunder. Copies of said Warrant Agreement are on file at the office of the Warrant Agent and the Company shall not be required to issue fractions of shares of Common Stock on the exercise of this Warrant but shall make adjustment therefor in cash on the basis of the current market value of any fractional interest (computed as provided in said Warrant Agreement) or, at its option, shall issue scrip in lieu thereof, all as provided in said Warrant Agreement.

In the event that this Warrant shall not be exercised on or before March 15, 1981, this Warrant shall become void and all rights hereunder shall cease.

This Warrant is transferable at the corporate trust office in the City of New York of the Warrant Agent (or of its successor as Warrant Agent) by the registered holder hereof or his assigns, in person or by attorney duly authorized in writing, but only in the manner and subject to the limitations provided in the Warrant Agreement, and upon surrender of this Warrant. Upon any such transfer, a new Warrant, or new Warrants of different denominations, of like tenor and representing in the aggregate the right to purchase a like number of shares of the Company's Common Stock will be issued to the transferee in exchange for this Warrant.

This Warrant when surrendered at the corporate trust office in the City of New York of the Warrant Agent, or of its successor as Warrant Agent) may be exchanged, in the manner and subject to the limitations provided in the Warrant Agreement, for another Warrant, or other Warrants of different denominations, of like tenor and representing in the aggregate the right to purchase a like number of shares of the Company's Common Stock.

Certificate or certificates for shares of the Company's Common Stock shall be deemed to have been issued (pursuant to the provisions of this Warrant and of the Warrant Agreement) and any person so designated to be named therein shall be deemed to have become a holder of record of such shares as of the date of the surrender of this Warrant, and payment of the Warrant price and any applicable taxes; provided, however, that if, at the date of surrender and payment of such Warrant price and taxes, the transfer books for the Company's Common Stock or other class of stock purchasable upon the exercise of this Warrant are closed for any purpose, the certificate for the shares in respect of which this Warrant is then exercised, shall be issuable as of the date on which such books shall next be opened and until such date, the Company shall be under no duty to deliver any certificate for such shares.

Nothing contained in this Warrant shall be construed as conferring upon the holder hereof any rights whatsoever of a Stockholder of the Company.

This Warrant shall not be valid unless countersigned by the Warrant Agent.

WITNESS the facsimile seal of McCrory Corporation and the facsimile signatures of its duly authorized officers.

Dated:

COUNTERSIGNED:
CHEMICAL BANK NEW YORK TRUST COMPANY,
WARRANT AGENT,

BY

SPECIMEN

AUTHORIZED SIGNATURE

McCARRY CORPORATION

BY

SPECIMEN

_____
CHAIRMAN OF THE BOARD

ATTEST:

Seymour Greene

SECRETARY

CORPORATE SEAL 1915 DELAWARE

Figure 3–3b. A Warrant (back)

ELECTION TO PURCHASE

(To be executed if owner desires to exercise the Warrant.)

To **McCarry Corporation**

The undersigned hereby irrevocably elects to exercise the right of purchase represented by the within

Warrant for, and to purchase thereunder, ... shares of the stock provided for

therein, and requests that certificates for such shares shall be issued in the name of ....

PLEASE INSERT SOCIAL SECURITY OR OTHER
IDENTIFYING NUMBER

....
(Please print name and address)

and, if said number of shares shall not be all the shares purchasable thereunder, that a new Warrant

for the unexercised portion of the within Warrant be registered in the name of ....

....
(Please print name and address)

....

Dated: ...., 19........

Signature: ....

NOTE: The above signature must correspond with the name as written upon the face of this Warrant or with the name of the person to whom this Warrant has been duly assigned in every particular, without alteration or enlargement or any change whatever, and if signed by an assignee, or if shares and/or Warrants are to be issued in a name other than that of the registered holder of the Warrant, the form of assignment hereon must be duly executed. If shares and/or Warrants are to be issued in a name other than that of the registered warrant holder, this election to purchase must be accompanied by appropriate documentary stamp taxes.

ASSIGNMENT

(To be executed if owner desires to transfer Warrant Certificate.)

FOR VALUE RECEIVED ....hereby sell, assign and transfer unto

....

....

the within Warrant, together with all right, title and interest therein, and do hereby irrevocably constitute and appoint

.... Attorney,

to transfer said Warrant on the books of the within-named Corporation, with full power of substitution in the premises.

Dated: ...., 19........

....
(Signature)

NOTE: The above signature must correspond with the name as written upon the face of this W   at in every particular, without alteration or enlargement or any change whatever. The signature to the Assignment must be guaranteed by a commercial bank or trust company having an office or correspondent in New York City or by a firm having membership in the New York Stock Exchange or in the American Stock Exchange Clearing Corporation.

Signature Guaranteed:

....

Figure 3–4. A Rights Certificate

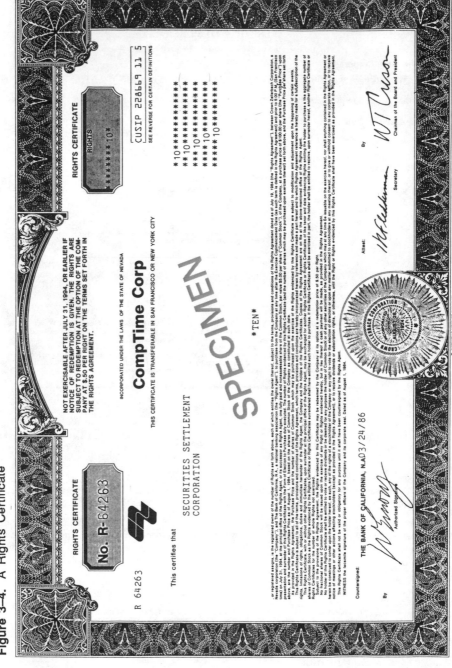

RIGHTS CERTIFICATE

No. R-64263

R 64263

This certifies that

SECURITIES SETTLEMENT
CORPORATION

NOT EXERCISABLE AFTER JULY 31, 1994, OR EARLIER IF
NOTICE OF REDEMPTION IS GIVEN. THE RIGHTS ARE
SUBJECT TO REDEMPTION AT THE OPTION OF THE COM-
PANY AT $.50 PER RIGHT ON THE TERMS SET FORTH IN
THE RIGHTS AGREEMENT.

INCORPORATED UNDER THE LAWS OF THE STATE OF NEVADA

CompTime Corp

THIS CERTIFICATE IS TRANSFERABLE IN SAN FRANCISCO OR NEW YORK CITY

SPECIMEN

TEN

RIGHTS CERTIFICATE

RIGHTS

*********10*

CUSIP 228669 11 5

SEE REVERSE FOR CERTAIN DEFINITIONS

*10***************
10************
10*********
****10***********
*****10**********

Countersigned:

THE BANK OF CALIFORNIA, N.A. 03/24/86

By

Authorized Signature

Attest:

Secretary

By

Chairman of the Board and President

To illustrate: Gyro International, whose common stock is trading at $35 per share, issues warrants that permit the owner to purchase stock at $60 a share any time up to December 31, 1997. If Gyro is a good growth company and the public perceives the common shares could not only reach the price of $60 by 1997 but could trade above that price, the warrants will make an attractive acquisition.

Warrants are usually issued with bonds or preferred stocks to make the initial public offering of these securities more attractive. As bonds must pay interest and preferreds pay a stipulated rate of dividend, both of which are paid before the common stockholders receive their dividends, the issuance of warrants may permit the corporation to offer either bonds or preferred stock at a reduced payment rate, thereby saving the corporation expense.

Warrants and the underlying stocks or bonds generally come to the marketplace as part of a *unit,* which is comprised of two or more issues. For example, a corporation may issue a combination of bonds and warrants. The bonds are in regular form, and the warrants are used to make the offering more attractive. If the issuing company is growth-oriented, with a track record of accomplishing its goals, the warrants will attract investors.

Because of the length of time that warrants are outstanding, a corporation can have several different warrants outstanding at one time. The value of each issue is determined by the relationships among several factors: the conversion price, the time remaining in the warrant, and the value of its underlying stock.

The Certificate

In the case of either a right or a warrant, the *certificate* itself is referred to as *a* right or *a* warrant. Actually, "a" right certificate could represent 100 rights, and "a" warrant certificate could represent 100 warrants. This term causes confusion and is a constant cause of errors in the brokerage community.

To illustrate: A company issues a unit comprised of a $1,000 bond with a warrant to purchase 10 shares of stock. When the parts of the unit are separated, the bond and the warrant sell separately. At that time, the warrant certificate represents 10 warrants—one per each share of stock.

Operations personnel should *always* make certain of whether the term means the right or warrant certificate *or* the quantity of rights or warrants represented by the certificate.

4   Corporate Bonds

Not only do corporations issue securities representing ownership, they raise capital also through the issuance of debt. Their debt securities may be long term, known as *bonds,* intermediate term, known as *notes,* or short term, known as *commercial paper.* Corporations also borrow money from banks. This form of financing is known as a *commercial loan.*

Market conditions, the wish not to dilute ownership, and many other reasons may lead a corporation to decide against issuing shares of stock to raise capital. Instead, it borrows money from the public sector in the following ways:

- A corporation borrows long-term capital through debt securities known as *bonds.* We speak of a corporation issuing or selling bonds. Actually, what the corporation is doing is borrowing money from the purchasers of these bonds in return for interest.
- A corporation borrows intermediate-term financing through *notes.*

- A corporation arranges short-term financing, referred to as *commercial loans,* through commercial banks. (Some corporations, especially finance corporations, issue a short-term instrument known as *commercial paper.*)

A corporation does not usually sell bonds when it wants to obtain only small amounts of working capital. Neither does the corporation sell its bonds to raise money that will be needed for a short time. A corporation can raise such funds less expensively by borrowing from a bank or by obtaining trade credit from its suppliers.

However, corporations sell bonds when they want to borrow large amounts of money to finance their long-range needs. For example, a corporation may sell bonds when it wants to build a new plant or to buy new equipment and machinery.

Corporations can issue many kinds of bonds and for many purposes. Before we discuss these bonds, however, let us take a look at what a bond is and how it differs from stock.

WHAT IS A BOND?

Briefly, a *bond* is a promise in writing (1) to pay a specific sum of money, (2) at a definite date in the future, and (3) with interest at a fixed rate and on specified dates. Figure 4–1 is a specimen bond. Although a corporation may issue different kinds of bonds, all bonds have the following things in common.

Face Value

On the front of the bond, there is usually a statement of the amount the corporation has promised to pay the holder of the bond. This amount is called the *face value* or *face amount* of the bond. Bonds may be issued in face amounts ranging from $50 to $10,000. The most common face amount is $1,000.

Figure 4-1. A Specimen Bond

Maturity Date

Also on the front of the bond is the *maturity date.* This is the date on which the corporation will pay back the face amount to the bondholder. This date is also called the *due date* of the bond. Maturity dates of corporate bonds vary, ranging up to 30 years or more.

Interest Rate

Each bond also contains a promise by the corporation to pay the bondholder a fixed rate of interest on specified dates. The rate of interest is usually stated as a percentage of the face amount of the bond. Although the interest rate is stated as a yearly rate, it is normally payable semiannually (twice a year). The interval may be

J&J	=	January - July
F&A	=	February - August
M&S	=	March - September
A&O	=	April - October
M&N	=	May - November
J&D	=	June - December

Purchase Price

Notice that the purchase price of a bond is stated as a percentage of the face amount. If the purchaser pays the face amount, we say he has paid 100%, or *par* for the bond. However, if he has paid more than the face amount—for example, 102%—then we say he has paid a *premium* for the bond. On the other hand, if he has paid less than the face amount—for example, 98%—then we say he has bought the bond at a *discount.* But whether the purchaser has paid par or a premium or a discount for the bond, the interest will always be figured on the face amount of the bond. Also, at maturity, the bondholder will be paid the face amount of the bond.

To illustrate: You buy a $1,000 bond, with a 5% interest rate, at 98%. This means you will have paid

$980 for the bond. But you will receive interest figured at 5% of $1,000, or $50 each year. Also, if you hold the bond to maturity, you will receive the face amount, or $1,000, not the $980 that you paid for the bond.

HOW BONDS DIFFER FROM STOCK

Bonds differ from stock in several ways:

1. A stockholder is a *part owner* in the corporation. The certificate of stock is evidence of his ownership. The bondholder, however, is a *creditor* of the corporation that has issued the bond. The bond itself is evidence of the debt owed him by the corporation.

2. The bondholder receives *interest* on the bond. This interest is fixed and definite. It must be paid before the corporation can declare or pay a dividend on its outstanding stock.

   If the corporation fails to pay the interest when it is due, this may *accelerate the maturity date* of the bond. To accelerate the maturity date means that the bondholders may demand the corporation pay them the face amount of their bonds at once.

   Also, failure to pay the interest may result in the corporation's being placed in receivership or being reorganized.

   On the other hand, a stockholder normally receives a *dividend*. A dividend is not fixed and need not be paid on specified dates. If the corporation decides not to declare or pay a dividend the stockholders can't do anything about it; they are bound by the corporation's decision.

3. Like any other creditor, the bondholder normally has no voting rights and so no voice in the management of the corporation. The stockholder, on the other hand, votes for the board of directors

and so has a voice in the management of the corporation.

TYPES OF CORPORATE BONDS

Corporate bonds may take many different forms:

Bearer Bond

The name of the owner of a bearer bond is not registered with the issuing corporation. Because of this we say that the bond is payable to the *bearer*—that is, to the person who has possession of the bond.

Bearer bonds have coupons attached. The bondholder clips a coupon on the interest date and sends it to the corporation's agent for payment. Bearer bonds are also known as *coupon* bonds.

Bearer bonds are rarely, if ever, issued any longer, However, there are still older issues in circulation.

Registered Bond

The name of the owner of a registered bond is registered (listed) with the issuing corporation. The holder of a registered bond does not have to send in coupons to the paying agent to receive his interest. Instead, the agent on the due date will automatically mail him a check for the interest.

Serial Bond

Rather than have the total amount of a bond issue become due on a specified date, some corporations like to arrange for portions of the bond issue to become due and payable in different years. For example, the corporation may arrange that bonds numbered from 1 to 100 will become payable in the fifth year after they are issued. Bonds numbered from 101 to 200 will mature in the sixth year, and so on. Such bonds are known as *serial bonds.*

Callable Bond

Some corporations include in their bonds a clause giving the corporation a right to call in (redeem) the bonds before the maturity date. Usually, the corporation agrees to pay the bondholder a *premium* (that is, more than the face amount of the bond) when it calls in the bond.

Convertible Bond

A convertible bond is similar to convertible preferred stock. The convertible bond gives the owner the right to exchange his bond for some other kind of security. This may be either the preferred stock or common stock of the issuing corporation. Many companies issue bonds that are convertible into stock because it makes the bond more attractive and so more readily saleable.

Sinking Fund

A sinking fund bond obligates the issuing corporation to set aside each year from its earnings a certain sum of money to be used to retire (pay off) the bond issue. Under this *sinking fund* provision, the corporation turns over the funds to the trustee for the bond issue. The trustee, in turn, uses it to retire a portion of the bond issue. In this way, the issuing corporation is able to pay off its debt a little at a time.

Secured Bonds

Like any other borrower, a corporation often puts up something of value as a pledge for its borrowings. When the corporation does this, we say it has issued a *secured* bond. Bonds may be classified according to how they are secured.

For example, a corporation may pledge a building or land that it owns. If later the corporation should default (fail to pay) the bonds, then the bondholders can take over and sell the building or the land. Also, if the corporation does not pay the interest on the bonds, then the bondholders may have the right to take over the building or land and sell it.

The major kinds of *secured* bonds are (1) mortgage bonds, (2) collateral trust bonds, and (3) equipment trust certificates.

Mortgage Bonds. A mortgage bond is similar to the ordinary real estate mortgage that a person gives to a bank to secure the payment of a loan on a home.

The corporation's mortgage may cover specific property (for example, a new plant). Or it may be a general mortgage on all the property owned by the corporation, including property that it will later acquire. Most corporate mortgage bond issues are of the general variety.

Collateral Trust Bond. When a collateral trust bond is issued, the issuing corporation puts up negotiable securities (stock and bonds) that it owns of other corporations. These securities are called the *collateral.*

The corporation deposits this collateral with a third party, usually a trust company. Of course, the value of the collateral is greater than the face amount of the bonds that the corporation issues.

Equipment Trust Certificate. The equipment trust certificate, which is a type of bond, is used mainly by railroads. It is secured by the railroad's rolling stock (passenger cars, freight cars and engines) and other standard equipment of the railroad. A certain portion of the bond issue is paid off each year. This results in increasing the security available for the remaining bondholders.

Unsecured Bonds

In much the same way that a person with a good credit rating can borrow without pledging any property, so too can a corporation.

If a corporation has a good credit rating, it can issue bonds on its name only. These bonds are called *debentures,* and the corporation pledges no specific property as security for them. Although nothing tangible secures the issue, the possibility of default is believed to be nonexistent because of the strength and good name of the issuer. To make the debentures more attractive, the corporation often may add a conversion feature (discussed earlier). These debentures are then known as *convertible debentures.*

BANK-ISSUED DEBT SECURITIES

Banks come to the marketplace primarily with two short-term instruments and one long-term instrument. *Certificates of deposit* (CDs) and *banker's acceptances* (BAs) are short term. CDs provide the banks with funds to make short-term loans. BAs are issued to assist in the financing of international trade. Banks also seek long-term funds in the financing of mortgages. They pool, or package, a group of mortgages and sell a security against them known as *participating certificates* (PCs).

5　Government and Municipal Debt Securities

U.S. TREASURY BILLS, NOTES, AND BONDS

Part of the Federal Reserve Board's role is providing the financing for the United States government through the issuance of three forms of securities:

1. Short-term instruments known as *U.S. Treasury bills (T bills)*.
2. Intermediate financing called *U.S. Treasury notes (T notes)*.
3. Long-term financing in the form of *U.S. Treasury bonds (T bonds)*.

Collectively, these instruments are known as *U.S. government securities.* Some of them trade on the New York and American Stock Exchanges, but most of them trade over the counter. All these instruments are direct obligations of the United States government and, as such, are considered to be among the safest investment vehicles available. They are generally backed by the full faith and credit of the federal government.

The Fed brings these instruments to the market through an *auction.* U.S. government *primary dealers,* which are privately owned firms registered as dealers, bid for the issues. Although only government dealers can compete in the auction market, the public can purchase U.S. treasuries directly from the Fed by submitting requests. Their orders are filled at an average price, formulated from the accepted dealers' bids.

T Bills

U.S. treasury bills are short-term instruments. The longest maturity is one year, the most popular being the 3-month and 6-month issues. Bills are discounted instruments. Discounted instruments usually do not have a fixed interest rate. Instead, the bills are bought at one amount and you receive a higher amount (the face value) at maturity. The difference between the two dollar amounts is the *discount.* The rate of interest earned is "built into" the discount.

T Notes and T Bonds

U.S. treasury bonds and notes are longer-term instruments than are T bills. Notes are issued for 1 to 10 years. Bonds are issued with maturities ranging from 10 to 30 years. Bonds and notes have fixed interest rates and pay interest on a semiannual basis. The instrument is computed on a 365-day basis, not 360 (as with bills and other instruments).

Settlement of U.S. Treasury Securities

In newer issues of U.S. treasuries, transactions are settled through the Fed's *book entry system,* that is, delivery is effected through computer entry rather than physical delivery. The Fed maintains the nominee name and address, and debits or credits the appropriate accounts as transactions are made. This method of settlement is fairly new. As a result, many of the older instruments must still be settled through physical delivery.

MORTGAGE-BACKED SECURITIES

GNMAs

GNMAs, sometimes known as *Ginnie Maes,* are debt instruments that are issued by Government National Mortgage Association (GNMA) and that represent pooled mortgages. The GNMA issues mortgages and receives interest payments. The money for those mortgages comes from investors who buy GNMA bonds. When the GNMA pays interest to its bondholders, the payments come from the pooled interest payments of the mortgage holders. The interest and principal payments are passed through the GNMA. Ginnie Maes are therefore called *pass-through certificates.*

Although the Government National Mortgage Association guarantees prompt payment of principal and interest on its bonds, the pooled mortgages comprising the GNMA issue are insured by various federal agencies. Mortgages backed by the federal government can be insured by the Veterans Administration (VA) or guaranteed either by the Federal Housing Authority (FHA) or by Farmers Home Administration (FmHA). Because the mortgages in a GNMA pool are backed by the U.S. government, they are an attractive investment.

Other Mortgage-Backed Securities

GNMAs have been joined by issues of the Federal Home Loan Mortgage Corporation (FHMA) called Freddie Macs, issues of the Federal National Mortgage Association (FNMA) called Fannie Maes, and issues of the Student Loan Association (SLA) called Sallie Maes. Each of these securities is pass-through, like Ginnie Maes.

Trading Mortgage-Backed Securities

Pass-through securities are traded in the over-the-counter marketplace among dealers, brokers, and dealer brokers. A round lot is $1,000,000, with odd lots being as small as $25,000.

MUNICIPAL BONDS AND NOTES

Municipal bonds, or *munis,* are debt instruments issued by state and local governments and their agencies to raise capital to finance their projects and other needs. Income (that is, interest) earned on municipal securities is free from federal income tax (that is, they are *tax exempt*). For a resident of the issuing municipality, interest from the bonds is also exempt from state and local income taxes.

Trading Municipals

When municipal bonds are issued, brokerage firms buy the issue from underwriters for resale to their customers. Most of the trading in munis takes place at this time, because purchasers usually buy these securities for investment purposes, not for ongoing trading. Muni buyers generally buy these bonds, hold on to them, and look forward to the tax-free interest payments.

Typically, therefore, individual municipal issues are traded infrequently, or *thinly.* That is why they are more suitable for trading on the OTC market than on exchanges. That is also why they are *not* quoted on a dollar basis, as are corporate bonds, whose issues trade frequently throughout their lifetimes.

So, except for a few muni issues, it is difficult to acquire a municipal bond in the *secondary market* (that is, the OTC market) in which these securities are resold. Someone who invests municipal bonds in the OTC market selects from an inventory maintained by a municipal bond dealer.

Kinds of Municipal Bonds

General obligation bonds are secured by the full taxing power of the issuing state or local government. Money to pay interest and principal comes from general tax revenues.

A *limited tax* bond is backed by a particular tax, such as a state sales tax.

Revenue bonds are secured by the revenue from the project built by capital raised in the bond issue. For example, the proceeds of a bond issue might be used to build an energy plant. Revenue from the sale of energy then pays back the bondholders.

There are other types of bonds, and their backing naturally affects their marketability.

Municipals may also be categorized according to their time of maturity.

Municipal Notes

State and local authorities often issue short-term instruments in anticipation of a need for capital. These instruments, known as *notes,* usually exist for six months or less. Notes issued in anticipation of taxes to be received are *tax anticipation notes* (TANs). Those issued in the expectation of future revenue are *revenue anticipation notes* (RANs). Those offered just before a new bond offering are called *bond anticipation notes* (BANs).

TANs, RANs, and BANs are usually *discounted instruments.* Holders receive no interest payments. Instead, buyers pay a price that is lower than (or discounted from) the full face value, which they are paid at maturity. The difference between the price paid at time of purchase and the sum received at maturity is the interest earned.

6   Other Instruments

Several other types of financial instruments need to be discussed briefly.

MUTUAL FUNDS

Mutual funds are managed companies that pool money obtained from the public to try and achieve certain investment goals. Most mutual fund companies have different types of funds available to the investment public. They may range from very aggressive to very conservative, from growth to income type offerings. All of the types of funds offered by one company are known as a *family of funds.*

OPTIONS

Option contracts permit holders to buy (in the case of a *call* option) or to sell (if a *put*) some underlying instrument, such as a stock, over a period of time at a specific price. At the end of an option's life, it expires.

Should the owner of the issue decide to exercise the contract, the seller of the option must perform the terms of the contract—either buy or sell at the contract price. For this option the buyer (owner) pays the seller (obligator) a premium at the time of purchase.

FUTURES CONTRACTS

Futures contracts provide for the delivery of a specified amount of a particular commodity during a specified future month, but they in fact involve no immediate transfer of ownership of the commodity. In other words, you can buy and sell commodities in a futures market regardless of whether or not you have, or own, the particular commodity. Basically remember this about buying and selling futures:

1 . When you *buy* a futures contract, you are *going long.* In so doing, you are simply agreeing to receive delivery and to pay in full for a specific amount and grade of a particular commodity to be delivered to you at a specific place in some designated month in the future.

2 . Conversely, when you *sell* a futures contract, you are *going short.* You are agreeing to deliver a specific quantity and grade of a particular commodity at a specific place in some month in the future, at which time you will be paid in full.

The terms and conditions of a futures contract are uniform: the size, the deliverable grades, the place of delivery, and many other specifications are all predetermined and detailed in the rules of the exchange. Consequently, when a contract is negotiated, the seller and buyer need settle on only the month of delivery, the number of contracts (or bushels, if grain), and the price. Price is determined by the competitive bidding and offering, by public outcry, on the floor of the organized futures exchanges.

Contracts may be filled by either delivery or offset. Fulfillment by *delivery* obviously means you either accept or deliver the goods, as contracted. Actually, however, only roughly 2% of all futures contracts are ever settled by deliveries. For the most part, they are *offset* (or liquidated) prior to the delivery month. Despite the contract, delivery is *not* mandatory; the participant in the market does not have to take or make delivery unless he or she is able and wishes to. The holder of a contract, either the buyer or seller, has the option of offsetting the contract. Offsetting is accomplished quickly and easily by simply selling or buying a contract of similar size in the same delivery month. For example, a speculator who has purchased, say, one contract of cotton can offset the contract by *selling* another contract of cotton in the same delivery month. Similarly, the one who has sold a contract can offset it simply by buying another contract of equal size and in the same month. Either way, one position cancels out the other, and the difference between the prices of the two transactions represents the speculator's profit or loss. Amazingly, the speculator can offset a position without regard for the other party originally involved in the contract, because at the end of each trading day the *clearing house* assumes the role of the "other party" for *all* transactions by its members. This responsibility on the part of the clearing house enables the participants to buy and sell contracts freely without regard to legal problems normally involved in the "breaking" of a contract. The chapter on clearing houses, later in this book, explains the vital role the clearing house plays in greater detail.

7   The Exchanges

The chief markets for trading in securities in this country are the organized securities exchanges and the over-the-counter (OTC) market. We commonly call the exchanges *stock exchanges,* even though stocks, bonds, commodities, options, and futures are traded there.

The two major stock exchanges are the New York Stock Exchange (NYSE) and the American Stock Exchange (Amex). The requirements of the New York Stock Exchange are more stringent of the two. On this exchange you find the common stocks of major national and international corporations.

Although the listing requirements of the American Stock Exchange are not quite as strict as those of the NYSE, the Amex-listed securities are nevertheless those of well-known corporations. These companies, however, are usually younger or have smaller capitalization than those listed on the New York Stock Exchange.

For a long time, a security could be listed on only one of these two national exchanges, not both. If a security was listed on the NYSE, it could not be listed on the Amex—and vice versa. Nowadays the exchange rules covering this stipulation have come under review, and experiments in *dually listed securities* (those listed on both the Amex and the NYSE) are underway.

Regional exchanges trade a few of the securities traded on the NYSE and the Amex, in addition to the securities of local corporations. These exchanges include the Midwest Stock Exchange (MSE), Pacific Stock Exchange (PSE), Philadelphia Stock Exchange (PHLX), and the Boston Stock Exchange (BSE).

In 1973 a new type of exchange was created in Chicago. It was the first *options exchange,* and it was named the Chicago Board Options Exchange (CBOE). Following in the path of this pioneer are a number of stock exchanges that have added options to their product mix to offer more saleable products to the public.

Commodity futures, or *commods,* are also traded on specific exchanges. The Chicago Board of Trade and the Mercantile Exchange are only two such exchanges. For many years, futures contracts were taken out only on commodities: wheat, soybeans, pork bellies, and the like. Then they extended to include oil or precious metals. Today, given the unpredictability of interest rates, they are taken out on debt instruments, such as Treasury securities, and on foreign currencies, such as South African krugerrands.

Today, futures are traded on exchange floors by brokers and/or traders. *Brokers* execute orders for the benefit of others, that is, for the customers of firms. *Traders* execute transactions for their own accounts; they are speculators who own seats on the exchange.

WHAT IS A STOCK EXCHANGE?

A *stock exchange* is a private association of brokerage firms that are called *members.* A member is said to have a *seat* on the exchange. Some exchanges permit member firms to own seats that are registered in the firms' names with the firms' employees being assigned to the seats. Other exchanges require that the seats be registered in the names of individuals. The main purpose of an exchange is to provide a central meeting place for its member-brokers. This central meeting place is often called the *floor.* Here, the brokers can trade in securities.

Usually, the brokers trade in securities for the accounts of their customers. However, as we shall see, some members also trade for their own account.

It is important to remember that a stock exchange itself does not own any of the securities that are traded on its floor. Nor does the stock exchange itself buy or sell any of the securities traded on the exchange. Instead, the securities are owned either by the exchange's members or by their customers.

It is also important to remember that a stock exchange does not establish (fix) the price at which any security is traded on the exchange. The price is determined in a free and open auction kind of trading. The price depends on the demand for a security and the supply of that security at a particular time. In other words, if sellers of a stock are offering to sell more shares of that stock than buyers want to buy, the price of that stock will tend to go lower. On the other hand, if buyers want to buy more shares of a stock than sellers are offering to sell, the price of that stock will tend to go higher.

THE NEW YORK STOCK EXCHANGE

The New York Stock Exchange (NYSE) is the largest of the organized stock exchanges. It is popularly called the Exchange or the Big Board. The Exchange is located in downtown New York City. It is in the financial district, at Broad and Wall Streets.

The Administration of the NYSE

All important decisions are made by a board of directors. This board is made up of Exchange members, allied members, and even some nonmembers. Also, the Exchange decided to hire a president to carry out the decisions of the board of directors. The president is paid a salary for heading the Exchange. The man chosen president cannot be a member of the Exchange.

Among its power, the board of directors decides which securities may be traded on the Exchange. Securities approved by the board are said to be *listed* for trading on the Exchange. Once they are listed, the securities may be traded (bought and sold) on the floor of the Exchange by the members.

The board of directors may, however, delist a security. To *delist* a security means that the security can no longer be bought and sold on the floor of the Exchange by the members. Or the board may *suspend* trading in a security. This means that the members *cannot* trade in the security on the floor for a period.

The board has the right to examine the way in which Exchange members and member firms conduct their business. It may also look into their financial condition. Most important, the board has the right to punish members for violations of the Exchange's rules. It may make the member pay a fine. Or it may not allow him to trade on the Exchange for a certain period. And, if the violation is a very bad one, the board may expel the member, that is, take away his membership.

Membership

Only individuals can become members of the NYSE. And only members can buy and sell securities on the floor. A member of the Exchange is known as a *broker*. He is sometimes called a *floor broker*.

A member of the Exchange can get together with other persons and organize a *brokerage firm,* or *member firm.* To do this, he must get the approval of the Exchange.

And the Exchange will not give its approval unless all persons connected with the firm meet its standards, or requirements.

The member firm can be a partnership, in which case the Exchange member must be a partner. The member firm also can be a corporation. If it is a corporation, the broker must be a voting stockholder and director of the corporation. The other persons who join with the Exchange member to organize the member firm become *allied members* of the Exchange.

The member firm can accept orders to buy and sell for its customers those securities listed for trading on the Exchange. Usually, these orders will be executed by the firm's own broker. If he is too busy or is not available, however, the order can be executed by another broker.

Requirements for Membership

The New York Stock Exchange has very high standards, or requirements, for membership. *The reasons:* (1) All trading on the floor is oral, by word of mouth. Brokers do not make any written agreements. (2) The member firms handle tremendous amounts of money and securities that belong to their customers. Thus, it is important that Exchange members and the persons who work for member firms be honest and reliable.

A person who wants to become a *member* (broker) of the New York Stock Exchange must:

1. Buy a membership—more popularly called a *seat.*

2. Be approved by the board of directors.

Before the board approves an individual for membership, it carefully investigates his background and character. Also, the board requires that the individual have a number of years of experience in the securities business. And it makes him demonstrate his knowledge of the business by passing a written examination.

The *allied members*—that is, the partners or voting stockholders of a member firm—must also be approved by the board of directors. Here, too, before the board approves an allied member, it investigates the person's background, character, and experience in the securities business. It also requires him or her to pass a written examination on the securities business.

In addition, the board requires that the member firm being started have a specified minimum amount of capital. And the member firm must meet this minimum requirement at all times.

TYPES OF BROKERS

In Chapter 3, you learned the difference between a *broker* and a *dealer.* You will recall that a *broker* is a person who acts as an agent for his customers, and that he receives a commission for his services. Usually, members of the Exchange act as brokers and charge their customers a commission. The minimum amount of this commission is set by the firm.

To Illustrate: You want to buy 100 shares of XYZ common stock, which is traded on the Big Board. You go to a member firm and give them the order. (You can recognize a member firm from the words, "Member of the New York Stock Exchange," which appear under the firm's name.) The firm transmits your order to its broker on the floor. He in turn tries to execute the order (buy the shares) for you. If he is successful, you pay the brokerage firm the cost of the shares, *plus* its commission.

You might also have the firm sell some shares of stock for you. Then the firm would deduct its commission, the stamp taxes, and other fees from the sale proceeds. You would receive a check for the difference.

There are several kinds of brokers on the Exchange, depending on their activities, as we explain in the following pages.

Commission House Broker

Most members of the Exchange are partners (or voting stockholders and directors) in a member firm. The member firm is also known as a *commission house.* This is because it charges its customers a commission for its services. The broker-partner, who executes the orders of the firm's customers on the floor of the Exchange, is called a *commission house broker* or *floor broker.*

Two-Dollar Broker

A two-dollar broker is an Exchange member but is an independent broker. He does not belong to a member firm. He may own or lease his seat. He executes orders for any member firm that hires him. If a member firm's floor broker has more orders than he can handle, or if he is absent from the floor, then the firm will give some orders to the independent broker. The member firm pays the independent broker a fee for his services. At one time, the independent broker's fee was $2 for each 100 shares he bought or sold for a member firm. That's how he got the name *two-dollar broker.* Today, however, the independent broker's fee is usually more than $2.

Registered Floor Trader

Some persons buy a seat on the Exchange just to buy and sell securities for their own personal account. Such a person is called a *registered floor trader.* Generally, he does not belong to any member firm. Years ago, the primary occupation of registered traders was to trade for their own accounts in an attempt to make a profit. With the proliferation of rules and regulations, this privilege is now severely restricted. Today, *registered traders* either assist specialists as market makers or act as two-dollar brokers.

Specialist

Each security listed on the Exchange is traded at only one particular location on the floor. This location is called a *post.* At each *post,* there are several brokers known as *specialists.* Each of these *specialists* is assigned to a particular post by the board of directors of the Exchange. He buys and sell securities that have been assigned to him by the board of directors.

The specialist performs two main functions:

1. Executing orders.
2. Making markets.

Usually, orders given to him for execution are limited price orders (discussed in the example following). Here, the specialist acts as a broker and receives the usual floor brokerage fee, or commission, for his services.

To Illustrate: You go to a brokerage firm and give it an order to sell 100 shares of XYZ stock. However, you will sell your stock at only $100 or more a share. You will not accept a lower price. An order such as yours is called a *limited price order,* or *limit order.*

When the firm's broker goes to the post at which XYZ stock is traded, he finds that the market price is now $95 a share. Since the broker also has orders to execute for his firm's other customers, he cannot stay at the post to watch the price of XYZ stock. So he gives your order to the specialist in XYZ stock. The specialist will see that your stock is sold when the market reaches the price you are asking.

Another function performed by the specialist is to help *maintain an orderly market* in the stocks that have been assigned to him. Perhaps a stock in which he is the specialist has a great difference, or *spread,* between its bid and offer prices. This means that buyers of the stock want to pay a much lower price for the stock than the sellers will accept. The specialist will then bid or offer shares of this stock for his own account at prices midway in the spread. In this way, he lessens the spread between the bid and the offer prices. Because he is buying and selling for his own account in such a case, the specialist is acting as a dealer.

Bond Broker

In addition to the equity floor, the NYSE also has bond and option trading facilities. The members of the bond trading floor are either of the commission house or two-dollar broker type.

A bond broker is a member of the Exchange who specializes in buying and selling bonds for member firms. A firm's floor broker is kept busy executing orders in stocks. Thus, most firms send their customers' bond orders to a *bond broker,* who charges a fee for his services in the same fashion as a two-dollar broker.

Participants on the option floor are not members. They own or lease option trading rights, which reflect a special trading privilege. The option floor is comprised of option specialists, brokers and floor traders known as *competitive option traders* (COTs).

The Amex offers equity, options, and bonds also. Their members are specialists, commission house brokers, or two-dollar brokers. The Amex option floor also has several different types of floor traders.

Chicago Board Option Exchange offers listed options and offers trading in a market maker system. Their membership is comprised of brokers and market makers. In addition, exchange employees known as *order book officials* (OBOs) execute public limit orders that are entrusted to them.

The Pacific and Philadelphia Exchanges use equities specialist systems and have similar constituencies to the Amex. Pacific Option Trading is similar to the CBOE system.

ODD LOT TRANSACTIONS

Securities are traded in units called *lots*. Most of the stock or equity securities trade in lots of 100 shares. These are called *round lots*. The price of the stock is quoted at a dollar amount per share. For example, a price of "$74\frac{1}{2}$" means "$74.50 a share." The cost of 100 shares at this price would be $7,450 ($74.50 x 100).

A few securities trade in smaller lots. These securities are traded in *10-share lots.* Most securities on the Exchange therefore are 100 round lot trades, and few are 10-share trades.

The public may purchase or sell shares of stock that are less than a round lot. In the case of a 100-share round lot, a customer of a firm may trade 1 to 99 shares and in the case of a 10-share round lot, a customer may trade 1 to 9 shares. When the customer trades in quantities less than a round lot, the transaction is known as an *odd lot.*

Odd lots are traded on the NYSE and the Amex with the assistance of the specialists. The specialists execute customers' odd lot orders against their own inventory positions. Odd lot orders are executed by the specialists based on the execution prices of round lots.

For example, a customer of a firm enters an order to purchase 25 shares of XYZ at the market. The order is sent to the specialist making a market in XYZ. The specialist holds the order until a round lot trade takes place. The odd lot will be executed against the specialist position. The transaction may or may not include an odd lot differential.

The odd lot differential is a fee that some specialists charge for executing odd lot orders. It is usually $\frac{1}{8}$ of a point for odd lot transactions. The differential is added to the purchase price and subtracted from sell prices. An odd lot buy order being executed on a round lot transaction at 30 would cost $30\frac{1}{8}$ per share to the odd lot customer.

Odd lot transactions are executed on the NYSE and the Amex in similar fashions. Specialists on both exchanges execute the odd lot orders entered by the customer of the respective exchange's member firms.

LISTING SECURITIES FOR TRADING ON THE NYSE

The New York Stock Exchange trades only in *listed securities*. These are securities that have met the listing standards of the Exchange and so have been approved for trading by the board of directors.

To have its securities listed on the Exchange, a corporation files an application giving information about itself, along with a detailed description of the securities to be listed. The corporation also pays the Exchange a listing fee. In addition, the corporation must register the securities with the Securities and Exchange Commission.

TRADING ON THE NYSE

Securities are traded on the New York Stock Exchange in a huge room known as the *floor*. As you have already learned, each security is assigned to a particular *post* on the floor. The security can be traded at that post only. (On the outside of the post, or booth, is a price indicator that shows the most recent sale price for each stock traded there.)

When a broker wants to execute an order in a stock, he goes to the post where the stock is traded. There he tries to make a trade at the best possible price for his firm's customer. Under the rules of the Exchange, trading is done by bids and offers. These must be called out so that all brokers who want to trade can hear them. The highest bid and lowest offer are known as the quote.

A *bid* is the highest price a buyer is willing to pay for a stock. An *offer* is the lowest price at which a seller is willing to sell. Bids and offers are made in multiples of

$\frac{1}{8}$ of a point; that is, $\frac{1}{8}, \frac{1}{4}, \frac{3}{8}, \frac{1}{2}$, and so on. Each $\frac{1}{8}$ represents $\frac{1}{8}$ of a dollar a share, or $12\frac{1}{2}$ cents.

Here is a simplified example that shows how a trade takes place on the floor of the Exchange:

A broker has an order to buy 100 shares of XYZ stock at the market. (*At the market* means he has been told to buy the stock at the best possible price.) The broker goes to the post at which XYZ stock is traded. There he learns that the latest quote for XYZ stock is "$34\frac{1}{2}$–$34\frac{3}{4}$." This means that $34.50 a share is the highest price that a buyer is willing to pay, and that $34.75 a share is the lowest price at which a seller is willing to sell.

The broker could immediately accept the offer of $34\frac{3}{4}$ and so execute the order. However, he wants to buy the stock at the lowest possible price, so he calls out "$34\frac{5}{8}$ for 100." This is the shorthand way of saying the broker will buy 100 shares at a price of $34.625 a share. But he finds no one willing to sell at that price. The broker then decides to accept the offer to sell at $34\frac{3}{4}$. He shows his acceptance by calling out "take 100." This means that he will buy the 100 shares at $34.75 a share. With this, the trade ends.

It is interesting to note that the brokers do not exchange written contracts. Instead, each broker makes out his own memorandum, or note, of the trade. This shows the number of shares, the ticker symbol of the stock, and the price of the stock. It also includes the other member's badge number and the name of that member's brokerage firm. Each broker sends his memorandum to his own telephone clerk. The clerk then transmits the information to the brokerage firm.

THE AMERICAN STOCK EXCHANGE

The American Stock Exchange (Amex) is the second largest organized stock exchange in the country. It is more than 100 years old.

The American Stock Exchange began as an open air market on the sidewalks of New York City's financial district. In 1921, the *New York Curb Market,* as this exchange was then known, moved indoors to its present building.

In 1929, it changed its name from *New York Curb Market* to *New York Curb Exchange.* And in 1953, its name was again changed, this time to *American Stock Exchange* (Amex).

Administration

The organization and operation of the American Stock Exchange are like those of the Big Board. The policy-making functions are in the hands of a board of governors. This board is elected by the Amex members. It is made up of floor members, allied members, and some representatives of the public.

The American Stock Exchange also has a paid president. He serves as the chief executive of Amex and is responsible for carrying out the policies of the board. The president is not a member of Amex.

Requirements for Membership in the Amex

As on the Big Board, membership in the American Stock Exchange is restricted to individuals. Together with nonmembers, they may organize a member firm. Those who apply for membership in Amex and their associates must be approved by the board of governors. They must meet tests as to their character and their experience. Also, they must pass written examinations.

Trading on the Amex

Trading procedures on the Amex are generally similar to those on the New York Stock Exchange. Standards for listing securities for trading on the American Stock Exchange represent a basic difference between Amex and the Big Board. Generally, the listing standards of the American Stock Exchange are not as rigid as those of the New York Stock Exchange. Another difference is that the Amex permits trading in a few stocks known as "securities admitted to unlisted trading."

Like the New York Stock Exchange, the American Stock Exchange has several kinds of brokers. These brokers are classified by their activities on the exchange. However, the American Stock Exchange does not have special firms that act as odd lot dealers. Instead, the specialist in a particular stock acts as the odd lot dealer for that stock.

8   The Over-the-Counter Market

Unlike the exchanges, the over-the-counter (OTC) market has no central meeting place. Instead, the securities houses that trade in securities in this market do business with one another over a large network of telephones and teletype instruments. In this chapter, we look at the firms that do business in this market and how they operate.

THE NATURE OF THE OTC MARKET

All securities transactions except those that take place on an organized stock exchange are handled in the over-the-counter market. The OTC market is not located in any central place. Instead, it consists of thousands of securities houses throughout the country. These securities houses, called broker-dealers, buy and sell securities usually for their *own account*. When they trade this way they are doing business as a *dealer*.

However, a broker-dealer may also trade in the over-the-counter market as an *agent* of the customer, charging a commission for the service. When a broker-dealer acts as an agent, he is doing business as a *broker*.

Some OTC broker-dealers specialize in buying and selling a particular security, and they usually keep the security in their inventory. These broker-dealers are known as *market makers* because they "make a market" in the security. Another name for market maker is *trader*. When other broker-dealers receive orders from their customers, they turn to market maker firms for quotations and, eventually, to execute the order.

As dealers, market makers take positions in their specialty issues. Usually, several different dealer firms will "make a market" in a particular issue, and the individual traders may make markets in several issues at one time.

To "make a market," the dealer states the highest price at which he is willing to buy the issue (bid) and the lowest price he is willing to sell the issue (offer). The bid and offer comprise the trader's *quote*. The difference between the bid and offer is known as the *spread*.

To illustrate: Stone Forrest & Rivers is a multiproduct firm, participating in the over-the-counter market. One of its traders, Phil O. Dendrin, makes a market in Winnings Corp. common stock, as well as in some other common stock. Phil's current quote is $82-\frac{1}{4}$. The "82" refers to the price Phil is willing to buy at. The "$\frac{1}{4}$" translates into $82\frac{1}{4}$, which is the price Phil is willing to sell at. These prices apply to any firm wanting to transact business in Winnings Corp. common stock, as well as to Stone Forrest & Rivers' own customers.

Trading in securities in the OTC market takes place in many different places. Because of this, the exact size of this market is not known. However, the dollar value of securities traded in the OTC market is estimated to be many times greater than that on all the organized exchanges. Also the securities of more companies are traded in the over-the-counter market than are *listed* on the organized exchanges. And, even securities listed on a stock exchange can be traded in the OTC market. This is the so-called *third market.*

SECURITIES TRADED IN THE OTC MARKET

You have learned that trading in securities on a stock exchange is limited to *listed* securities. Generally, these are securities of national companies. A national company is a company whose securities are owned by many investors throughout the country.

In the over-the-counter market, however, the trading ranges from securities of large national companies to those of purely local companies. The securities of a local company are often owned by the residents of a particular town or city.

It is not unusual for a local business or industry to raise capital through the sale of its securities to residents of the community. Also, in order to attract business or industry to its community, the residents will buy a company's securities and so help it raise capital. A local broker-dealer will then buy and sell the securities.

Many different kinds of securities are traded in the over-the-counter market. These include bank stocks, insurance company stocks, U.S. government and municipal securities, mutual fund shares, railroad equipment trust certificates, most corporation bonds, securities of many industrial and utility corporations, and the securities of foreign corporations.

Keep in mind that almost all new issues of securities are first traded in the over-the-counter market. Later some of these securities may be *listed for trading* on a stock exchange. Many, however, will not be listed. These will continue to be traded in the OTC market.

BROKERS AND DEALERS

There is no such thing as a *seat* on the OTC market. *Any* securities house—proprietorship, partnership, or corporation—may do business in the OTC market.

However, there are these conditions: Before a securities house can do business as a broker-dealer, whether on the exchanges or the OTC market, it must register with the Securities and Exchange Commission. In addition, the broker-dealer and all persons connected with the broker-dealer (except clerical employees) must meet certain standards of training and experience. They must also pass a written examination.

OVER-THE-COUNTER FIRMS

An over-the-counter securities firm may do business in one particular part of the OTC market, or it may do business in all. An over-the-counter firm may be put in one of the following four categories:

1. Investment banking house.
2. Bond house.
3. Over-the-counter securities house.
4. Dealer's broker.

Investment Banking House

An investment banking house specializes in distributing new issues of securities. As you have learned, this type of firm is also called an *underwriter.*

When an investment banking firm distributes securities, it acts as a *dealer.* That is, the firm buys securities from the issuing corporation for its own account. It then tries to resell these securities at a higher price. The difference between the price at which it buys the securities and the price it sells them for is its profit.

Bond House

A bond house specializes in trading in U.S. government bonds, as well as state and municipal bonds. Some firms trade either in government bonds or in municipal bonds (munis). Other firms, however, may trade in both.

Bonds in the OTC Market. Municipal securities trade OTC because of their general *thinness* of issue, that is, the infrequency that a particular issue will trade. In most cases, most of the trading in a particular municipal bond occurs when it is first issued. After that, trading subsides, only to reappear sporadically during the issue's life.

Over-the-Counter Securities House

The over-the-counter securities house may be likened to the member firm that does business on an organized stock exchange. Another name for the over-the-counter securities house is *broker-dealer* firm.

The broker-dealer firm trades in over-the-counter securities for its customers. Generally, the broker-dealer firm will not trade in government and municipal bonds. It leaves that to the bond houses that specialize in these securities.

The larger broker-dealer firms may also act as underwriters for new issues of securities. But most often they act as dealers in the distribution of those securities, and later they will trade in them.

Dealer's Broker (Broker's Broker)

A certain type of brokerage firm has as its customers the many dealers and brokers trading in the marketplace. This type of firm is called a *dealer's broker* (or *broker's broker*). Firms inform a dealer's broker of what they are looking to sell or buy. The dealer's broker then communicates the request through a network to other participants.

To illustrate: The municipal trading desk of an OTC firm does not have any state of Oklahoma bonds in inventory, because the firm does not have a branch in Oklahoma and its public is not interested in that state's issues. To accommodate a sudden request to buy or sell munis of Oklahoma, the firm's trader could call either another firm that maintains a market in this security or a dealer's broker. The dealer's (or broker's) broker, with its extensive communication network, can give the trader and his customer's requirement full view in the marketplace, and the responses will give the firm and its client a better selection to choose from.

REGULATION OF THE OTC MARKET

You will recall that an organized stock exchange must register with the Securities and Exchange Commission. And the stock exchange must satisfy the Securities and Exchange Commission that it can properly police its members.

Regulation of the over-the-counter market works a little differently. Each broker-dealer firm must register with the Securities and Exchange Commission before it can do business in the OTC market.

In addition, there is an association of broker-dealer firms that is also registered with the Securities and Exchange Commission. This association is called the National Association of Securities Dealers, Inc. (NASD). It was created under a federal securities law. The purpose of the NASD is to adopt, administer, and enforce rules of fair practice in connection with transactions in the OTC market.

MEMBERSHIP IN THE NASD

Any broker-dealer firm registered with the SEC may become a member of the NASD. But membership in the NASD is not mandatory. This means that a firm may do business in the over-the-counter market without being a member of the NASD. However, a securities house that is not a member of the NASD comes directly under the supervision of the Securities and Exchange Commission.

Unless a securities house is a member of the NASD, it cannot get certain dealer discounts, especially those involving new issues of securities. To become a member of the NASD, a firm has to fill out and file certain application forms. It must send them to the NASD, together with a registration fee.

Like the organized stock exchanges, the NASD supervises the way in which its members do business. The NASD may censure, fine, or suspend a member firm if it breaks the rules. To suspend a member firm means that it cannot do business as a broker-dealer on the over-the-counter market for a specified period.

Another way the NASD can discipline a firm that has violated the rules is to revoke the membership. This, in effect, puts the firm out of business because members of the NASD can conduct trading business *only* with other members. A member who is suspended or whose registration is revoked may ask the Securities and Exchange Commission to review the NASD's decision.

TRADING IN THE OTC MARKET

You learned in Chapter 6 that a stock exchange is an auction market. That is, at the time that the highest bid and the lowest offer meet, a trade is made or executed.

Trading in securities in the OTC market works differently: Here the purchase and sale of securities is carried on by negotiation, or bargaining, between the parties. (Later in this chapter, we will show you how negotiation works.)

The over-the-counter market has no central meeting place. So there is no floor or post to which a broker-dealer can go to trade in over-the-counter securities.

THE MARKET MAKERS

However, the OTC market does have its *specialists* in securities. These are firms that have watched a new issue with great interest. They decide to become *market makers,* that is, they decide to buy the newly issued securities for their inventory and sell them for a profit. The market makers (also known as *dealers* or *traders*) are acting as *principals;* that is, they have committed their capital to the securities they are trading.

These firms *maintain a market* in a security. This means that the firm stands ready at all times to buy or sell a particular security, at prices the firm quotes. In these transactions, the firm usually acts as a *dealer.* A broker-dealer firm that maintains a market, or makes a market, in a security is known as a *market maker.*

The Bid and Asked

The market maker's quotation for a stock will consist of a bid price and an asked, or offer, price. The *bid* price is the highest price the market maker is willing to pay for a particular security. The *asked* price is the lowest price at which the market maker will sell a particular security. The difference between the bid and asked prices is called the *spread.*

To illustrate: The quote on ZAP is $45-\frac{1}{2}$. The bid, or price, is 45, or $45; this is the highest price someone is willing to buy the stock for, $45 per share. The offer is $45\frac{1}{2}$, or $45.50; it is the lowest current price at which anyone is willing to offer the security for sale. Whenever the bid and offer are equal, a trade occurs.

Quotations in the OTC Market

Due to the use of principal transactions in the OTC markets, quotes that are displayed on the automated quotation system screens (discussed later in the chapter) are known as *inside quotes.* These are the prices at which a broker-dealer will transact business before any markups or markdowns.

Depending on the depth of the market and the interest in the particular security, quotes may be firm, subject, or work-out.

- *Firm quotes:* The dealer is willing to transact business up to the size of the bid and offer. For a firm quote of $52\frac{1}{4}$–$\frac{1}{2}$ 8x5, the dealer will buy up to 800 shares at $52\frac{1}{4}$ or sell up to 500 shares at $52\frac{1}{2}$. Any more than the stated size must be negotiated.
- *Subject quotes:* A quote that is subject means that the market maker is making the bid or offer "subject" to verification with the contra side.
- *Work-out quotes:* Very inactive over-the-counter issues may require special handling of orders. As the liquidity is not present in the marketplace, the market maker would have to contact known interests in that issue and try to negotiate a transaction. The price at which a trade could occur is a management decision.

When a firm has chosen to process a non-market-making OTC security on a principal basis, the firm buys (or sells) the security against the dealer versus their trading account, and then buys or sells out of the trading account versus the customer.

To illustrate: A customer, M1345752, of SFR wants to purchase 100 shares of Dobrillus at the market. GRC has the best quote $49\frac{1}{2}$–$\frac{3}{4}$. SFR will purchase the stock at $49\frac{3}{4}$ for its trading account and turn around and sell it at $50\frac{1}{4}$ to its customer. In effect, the customer has been charged a $\frac{1}{2}$-point markup.

A *firm* price is the price at which a security can be bought or sold for such period of time as the seller may name. A *subject* price means that the price is subject to confirmation with the opposing side of the proposed transaction. A *work-out price* is given when the trader must shop around for interest in the possible execution of the trade.

How a Trade Is Made
in the OTC Market

So that you will better understand how a trade is made, or executed, in the OTC market, we have made up the following example:

Suppose you want to buy 100 shares of Golden Gondola common stock. This stock is traded on the over-the-counter market. You call Johns & Co., a broker-dealer firm, and give the order to the registered representative there who handles your account.

However, this firm does not *make a market* in Golden Gondola common stock. Because of this, the registered representative cannot give you an immediate execution on the stock. So he tells you that he will check the market and call you back. To *check the market* means that Johns & Co. will call several dealers who *make a market* in the stock. In this way it can get executions for you.

The first dealer, let's call him Dealer A, quotes the stock at "35–$35\frac{3}{8}$." In other words, Dealer A will buy Golden Gondola common at $35 a share and will sell it at $35.375 a share.

Another dealer, Dealer B, quotes the stock at "$34\frac{7}{8}$–$35\frac{1}{2}$." This means that Dealer B will buy Golden Gondola common at $34.875 a share. He will sell it at $35.50 a share.

Still another dealer, Dealer C, quotes the stock at "35–$35\frac{1}{2}$." In other words, this dealer will buy Golden Gondola common at $35 a share; he will sell it at $35.50 a share.

From these quotations, Johns & Co. knows that it can most likely buy Golden Gondola at the low price of $35.375 a share—the price quoted by Dealer A. On this basis, the registered representative calls you back and tells you that he can sell you 100 shares of Golden

Gondola common at, say, $36 a share. Johns & Co. added a *markup* of $0.625 a share to the price. This is the difference between the price it will pay for the stock and the price at which it will sell the stock to you.

From the foregoing description of this transaction, you recognize that Johns & Co. is acting as a *dealer*. However, there is nothing to stop Johns & Co. from acting as a *broker*. It would then charge you a commission for its services.

PUBLICIZING OTC QUOTATIONS

Because trades occurring on the exchanges are executed in a specific location, recording transactions for public display is relatively easy. Almost every branch of every brokerage firm has various types of video displays that reflect the executions taking place on the various exchanges. Other types of units display the last sale price, the opening price, and on and on. This feature of the listed trading market does not exist in the OTC market because trades are executed between firms through a telephone network.

The current market prices of the more popular OTC issues are found on various National Association of Security Dealer's Automated Quotation (NASDAQ) display systems. This system displays the current bid and offer on these securities. There are three levels of NASDAQ service. Level one is a representative quote comprised of the highest bid and lowest offer existing at that particular moment. It takes into account all the quotes existing with the market makers and displays a single quote for use by the public. Level two is used by the traders on the various firms' OTC trading desks. It displays all the market makers and their respective quotes. These data inform the traders who the market makers are and what their current quotes are. Level three is used by the market makers only. This level permits the market makers to adjust the quotes.

Through NASDAQ, the public is informed of the current market prices of OTC securities. Although

NASDAQ cannot give last sales or opening high and last, and so on, it can provide the current nominal quote.

Selected Quotations

Through its quotations committee, NASD gathers each business day the bid and asked prices on a selected list of over-the-counter securities. These quotations are released to about 300 newspapers throughout the country. These newspapers print these bid and asked prices daily.

A broker-dealer firm that belongs to the NASD may request his local quotations committee to include a particular security in the list of bid and asked prices. Whether the quotations committee honors the request depends to a great extent on how well the particular security meets the standards set by the committee.

The Pink Sheets

In addition, a private organization—the National Quotation Bureau—publishes what are known as the *pink sheets.* These sheets are published daily. They give the so-called *wholesale* quotations for over-the-counter securities.

These wholesale quotations are the prices at which dealers will buy and sell securities. Actually, they represent quotations of the dealers making a market in a security. Alongside each quotation, the pink sheet gives the name of the dealer or dealers involved. The pink sheets are not distributed to the public. They are distributed only to securities houses that subscribe for them.

9

Operations:
An Overview

The rest of this book follows a transaction from receipt at the brokerage firm through the operating processing cycle. In doing so, it attempts to show the various checks and balances used by firms in reconciling and controlling the many entries processed on a given day. The main operations functions are:

- *Order Room Function*—responsible for processing of orders and accurate reporting of executions.
- *Purchase and Sales Function*—trade figuration and the reconcilement of customer side vs. street side.
- *Margin Function*—insures that customers are maintaining their accounts in accordance with rules and regulations and firm policy.
- *Cashiering*—controls the movement of all securities and transaction-related funds into, out of, and within the firm.
- *Depository Function*—immobilization of certificates permits settlement via book entry.

- *Clearing Corporations Function*—expedites the comparison and settlement of transaction inter-firm.
- *Daily Cash*—makes final reconciliations of all fund movement and positions that the firm has a responsibility for.
- *Dividend/Bond Interest*—"books" and balances dividends and/or bond interest in customer and proprietary accounts.
- *Stock Record*—keeps up-to-date records of all securities for which the firm is responsible.
- *Proxy Function*—distributes issuer-originated documentation to beneficial owners whose issues are maintained by the firm.

All issues offered by the firm to its clients must go through these functions. While the instruments may have different settlement cycles, each transaction must be affected by this processing routine.

We will now go behind the scenes of a securities house. We will examine the operations of the various departments in what is popularly known as the *back office.* Our purpose is to find out who does what—and why, and how the jobs of the people around you fit in with your job.

The work of the operations division begins when a customer enters an order for the purchase or sale of securities. Figure 9–1 shows the organization of a typical operations organization and the flow of work through it. The heavily outlined boxes are areas within the firm. The lightly outlined boxes are agencies and companies outside the firm.

CUSTOMERS AND CUSTOMERS' ACCOUNTS

Who are the customers of a securities house? They are individuals, partnerships, corporations, and

Figure 9–1. A Typical Operations Organization. Reprinted with permission from David M. Weiss, *After the Trade Is Made* (New York: New York Institute of Finance, 1986).

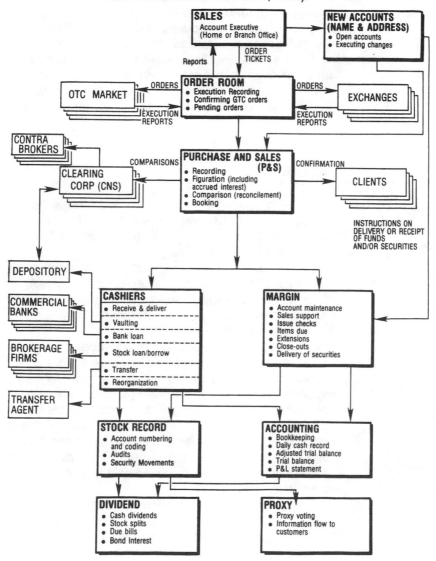

others who purchase or sell securities either for investment or for speculation.

Many securities houses have a main office in one city and a branch or branch offices in other cities. The customers may enter orders to buy or sell securities either through a branch office or the main office. However, before a customer can enter an order (do any trading), he must open an account with the securities house.

OPENING AN ACCOUNT

It is not difficult for a financially responsible person to open an account with a securities house. The procedure is basically similar to opening a charge account at a store or obtaining a credit card.

A person who wants to open an account must satisfy the firm that he is financially responsible. Also, the person must supply personal information such as name and address, age, Social Security number, and investment objectives.

An account is usually opened through one of the firm's registered representatives. A *registered representative* is an employee of a securities house. He or she accepts orders for the purchase and sale of securities from the firm's customers and also deals with them on other matters. Such a person must have a good knowledge of the securities business and has to pass a written examination. The registered representative may also be called an *account executive* or a *customer's broker.*

After an account has been opened, it is assigned a code number and an account number. In addition, the customer's credit references will be checked. Also, a partner or officer of the firm will have to approve the account. Opening and maintaining the account is the work of the new accounts (or name and address) department.

A most important part of customer service is opening a new account properly. All of the salesmanship, the firm's reputation, and advertising can amount to nothing if the account has consistently misspelled a name or sent confirmations to the wrong address. Think about it: *You* probably are annoyed when someone calls you by the wrong name or when your mail is sent to someone else. Would you not think, "How important can I be to them if they can't even get my name or address right?" You may expect the same reaction among customers of the brokerage firm.

NEW ACCOUNTS

When opening the account, the customer indicates how he wants to do business, whether on a cash basis or a margin basis. Depending on his wishes and the firm's approval, he may either have a *cash* account or a *margin* account, or both.

Individual Cash Account

The simplest account to open is an *individual cash account,* in which only cash transactions may be executed and which is in the name of one person. First, the registered representative or the customer fills out a *new account form,* which requests the following information about the customer:

1. Full name.
2. Home address and telephone number.
3. Social Security number.
4. Occupation, place of employment, and business phone number.
5. Age, or date of birth.
6. Spouse's name and place of employment.
7. Bank reference.

Some firms require more detailed information as a matter of policy even though such information is not mandatory by law. Such additional information might include the following:

8. Annual income and net worth.

9. Number of children and their ages.

10. Accounts at other brokerage firms.

The completed form is filed in the new accounts department.

Some firms microfilm or microfiche each and every document. *Microfilm* is a reel of documents photographed at a great reduction. *Microfiche* is a sheet of documents, also greatly reduced. On either reel or sheet, you can store vast numbers of documents in a very small area. Viewers enlarge the filmed images, as needed, very much as a projector enlarges regular movie film. Prints can also be made at their original sizes from the film.

To keep track of the daily flood of documents, firms use a coding system, which identifies the reel of microfilm or sheet of microfiche on which the document is located. This code appears on the customer's *master file,* which is a file (either electronic or manual) that lists all current accounts by number, name, and address, or some other way.

Some firms also require customers to sign *signature cards* (usually two sets). These cards become permanent records of the customer's signature. One set is maintained in the branch, and the other is sent to the new account department.

When both of these forms are completed and all other requirements are satisfied, the customer may do business with the firm. Because this is a cash account, all securities purchased must be paid for on the *settlement* date, which is usually five full business days, but no later than the seventh business day, after the *trade* date.

The *trade* date is the date on which the purchase or sale is executed. The *settlement* date is the date on which the customer has agreed to settle the contract made for him by his broker.

Margin Account

A *margin* account is, in effect, like a credit account. The customer puts up part of the cash for his purchases; the broker then lends him the rest of the money.

To open a margin account, the new account form and (sometimes) the signature cards must be filled out. In addition, the customer must sign two other forms:

1. The *margin agreement* sets forth the terms under which the firm will lend money to the customer, the rules by which the account must operate, when the firm has the right to take action without the customer's permission, and the firm's right to charge interest on any *debit balance,* which is the amount of the loan. It also authorizes the broker to *liquidate* (that is, sell) sufficient securities out of the account in order to keep the account within the margin requirements.

2. The *lending agreement* gives the firm the privilege of lending the margined security to other firms or against other customers' short sales.

(Margin accounts are discussed more fully in Chapter 12.)

Joint Account

A *joint account* is an account in which two individuals, by legal agreement, may conduct transactions. It may be a cash or margin account. The two principal types are as follows:

1. *Joint Tenants with Rights of Survivorship* (or *Tenant by the Entirety*). This type of account is usually established between husband and wife. By this agreement, upon the death of one principal, the entire account reverts to the survivor.

2 . *Tenants in Common.* By this agreement, the death of one principal has no effect on the survivor's percentage of ownership in the account. The portion owned by the deceased reverts to his or her estate. In a tenants in common account, having the percentages of ownership on file is clearly important. In the absence of such a document, the account is automatically divided on a fifty-fifty basis.

Power-of-Attorney Account

Many times an account is managed not by the owner but by someone else. For this someone else to operate, the owner of the account must file a *power of attorney form,* of which there are two types, as follows:

1 . The *limited power of attorney* permits the person managing the account to enter buy and sell orders.

2 . The *full power of attorney* permits the person to deposit and withdraw securities and cash in addition to buying and selling securities.

Generally, for accounts handled under power of attorney, the brokerage firm must have the following papers on file:

1 . The usual papers for each owner.

2 . A power of attorney (limited or full) from each owner.

3 . A new account information form completed by the holder of the power of attorney.

Corporate Account

Before a corporation can purchase and sell securities, its charter must permit it to do so. Therefore, in addition to the usual papers connected with a corporate account, the brokerage firm must obtain a copy of the corporate customer's charter or bylaws.

Because a corporation is a legal entity, the brokerage firm must know who is empowered to act on the corporation's behalf. A *corporate resolution,* signed by the appropriate officers of the corporation, authorizes one or more of the company's officers to transact business in the corporation's name and for its benefit.

Other Accounts

There are other types of accounts—trust accounts, pensions, partnerships, and estates. The new accounts department is responsible for the followup that makes sure the accounts are opened properly. Individuals acting in a fiduciary capacity for such accounts must furnish *trust agreements, custodial agreements,* and similar documents completed and signed by notaries (where applicable).

10   The Order Room

Whether a security is traded over the counter or on an exchange, orders reflect the fact that buyers and sellers want to transact business. At any point in time, there is the highest price at which anyone is willing to buy and the lowest price at which anyone is willing to sell. These two interests make up the quote. The buyer with the highest price is said to have the "best" bid, whereas the seller with the lowest selling price is said to be the "best" offer. The *quote* is therefore comprised of the highest bid and lowest offer. The quantity representing the bid and/or on a quote vendors screen of the offer is known as the *size*. For example, a display of $37\frac{1}{2}$ 80x50 means that 8,000 shares are bid at 37 and 5,000 shares are offered at $37\frac{1}{2}$.

CUSTOMERS' ORDERS

The registered representatives of a securities house act as liaison between the customers and the firm. When a customer wants to buy or sell a security, he places his order with the registered representative who is handling his account. He may do this by telephone, personal visit, or letter. Most customers enter orders by telephone.

At one time, the registered representative sent all customers' orders for the purchase or sale of securities to the order department (also known as the *order room* or *wire room*). There an order clerk checked on which securities market (organized stock exchange or over-the-counter market) the security was traded. The clerk then sent the order to the appropriate marketplace to be executed.

Today, however, may securities houses have direct wires from their main offices and branch offices to the floors of the exchanges. So, in these firms, orders for the purchase or sale of listed securities are no longer sent to the order room. Instead, these orders are transmitted directly to the floor of the appropriate exchange.

The method by which orders are routed from the branch office to the point of execution is dependent on the firm's automated systems. Some firms have computer capabilities that run a series of programs known as *order match*. Contained in this system is a table of all of the issues and the location of where they are traded. Therefore, the branch office staff enters the order into the system, and the order is routed to the point of execution. Firms that do not have this type of system must rely on the branch personnel to designate on the order ticket the trading market to which the order is to be sent.

Other areas of the firm that can be a source of orders are the firm's trading desks, their arbitrage department, the syndicate departments, institutional trading area, and even orders for one product originating in the trading area of another product.

All customers' orders for the purchase or sale of *unlisted* securities are still sent to the order room. That's because *unlisted* securities are traded in the over-the-counter market only. You will recall that the OTC market has no central market place, or floor. Instead, all trading in the OTC market is conducted by telephone or teletype between the dealers who do business in this market.

Whether an order goes first to the order room or is sent directly to the floor of an exchange, the procedures for handling *all* customers' orders are practically the same: Someone must write out an order form (or type it into a terminal). The order must then be transmitted to the proper securities market to be executed. And if the order is executed, a report of the execution must be made.

THE ORDER FORM

The customer's instructions to buy or sell a security must be written out on an order form. This is usually done by the registered representative, but it may be done by a clerk. Figure 10–1 is a specimen order form.

Contents of the Order Form

Each order form must contain the following information:

1. Whether it is a *buy* or *sell* order. Generally, the words "buy" or "sell" are not written out. Instead, the letters "B" or "S" are used. Some securities houses use order forms on which the words "buy" and "sell" are already printed. On these order forms, the word "buy" is printed in black, and the word "sell" is printed in red.

2. If the order is a *sell* order, whether the sale is *long* or *short*. A *long* sale means the customer owns the security being sold. A *short* sale, on the other hand, means that the customer is selling a security he does not own but has borrowed. In a short sale, the customer believes the price of the security will drop. If it does, he then buys in the security at the lower price and returns the borrowed stock. His profit is the difference between the sales price and

Figure 10–1. A Typical Order Form

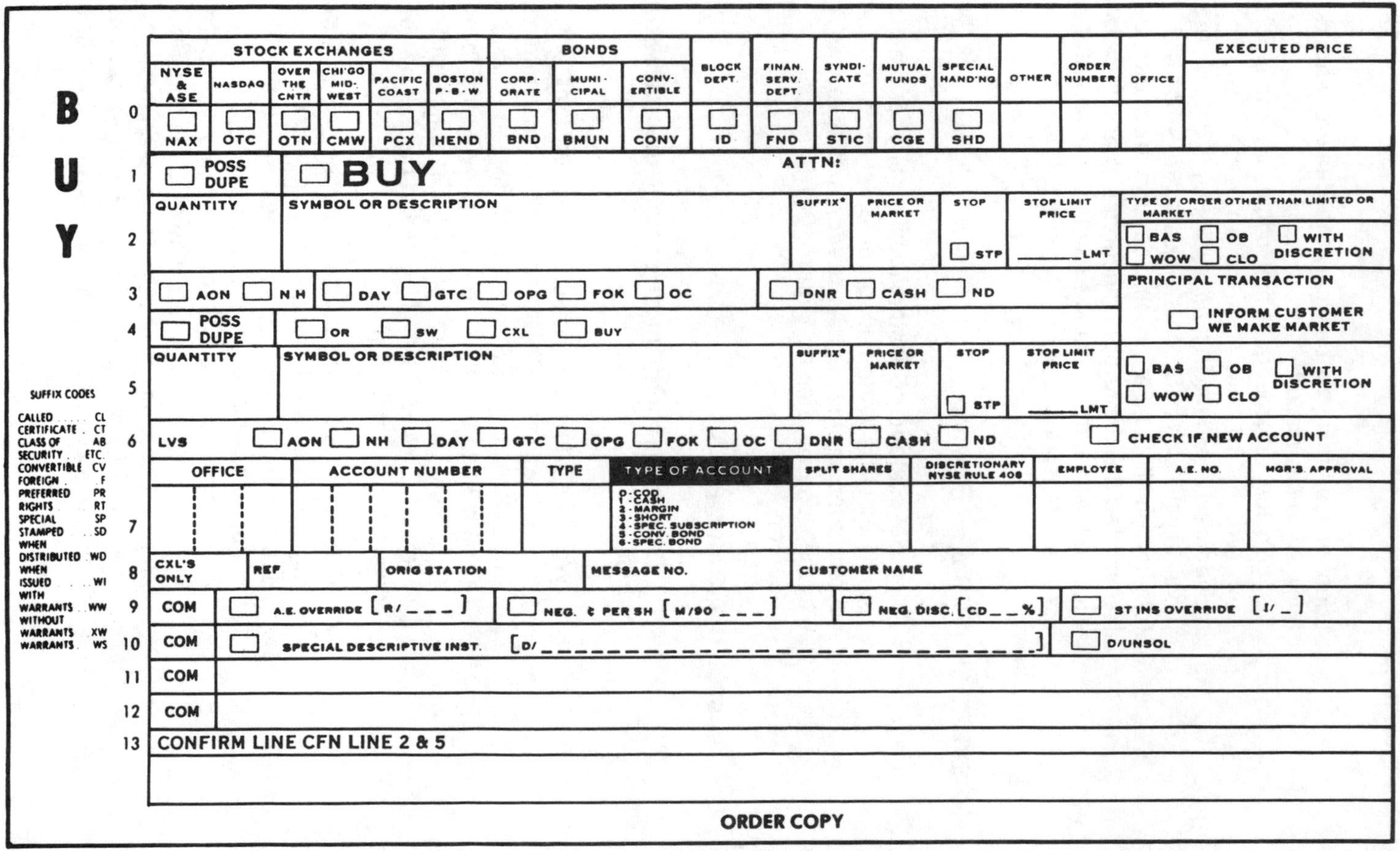

B U Y

SUFFIX CODES
CALLED CL
CERTIFICATE .. CT
CLASS OF ... AB
SECURITY .. ETC.
CONVERTIBLE CV
FOREIGN ..... F
PREFERRED ... PR
RIGHTS ..... RT
SPECIAL ..... SP
STAMPED .... SD
WHEN DISTRIBUTED . WD
WHEN ISSUED ..... WI
WITH WARRANTS .. WW
WITHOUT WARRANTS .. XW
WARRANTS .. WS

0 STOCK EXCHANGES: NYSE & ASE — NAX; NASDAQ — OTC; OVER THE CNTR — OTN; CHI'GO MID-WEST — CMW; PACIFIC COAST — PCX; BOSTON P-B-W — HEND
BONDS: CORP-ORATE — BND; MUNI-CIPAL — BMUN; CONV-ERTIBLE — CONV
BLOCK DEPT. — ID; FINAN. SERV. DEPT. — FND; SYNDI-CATE — STIC; MUTUAL FUNDS — CGE; SPECIAL HAND'NG — SHD; OTHER; ORDER NUMBER; OFFICE; EXECUTED PRICE

1 POSS DUPE; BUY; ATTN:

2 QUANTITY; SYMBOL OR DESCRIPTION; SUFFIX*; PRICE OR MARKET; STOP — STP; STOP LIMIT PRICE ______LMT; TYPE OF ORDER OTHER THAN LIMITED OR MARKET: BAS, OB, WITH DISCRETION, WOW, CLO

3 AON; N H; DAY; GTC; OPG; FOK; OC; DNR; CASH; ND; PRINCIPAL TRANSACTION

4 POSS DUPE; OR; SW; CXL; BUY; INFORM CUSTOMER WE MAKE MARKET

5 QUANTITY; SYMBOL OR DESCRIPTION; SUFFIX*; PRICE OR MARKET; STOP — STP; STOP LIMIT PRICE ______LMT; BAS; OB; WITH DISCRETION; WOW; CLO

6 LVS; AON; NH; DAY; GTC; OPG; FOK; OC; DNR; CASH; ND; CHECK IF NEW ACCOUNT

7 OFFICE; ACCOUNT NUMBER; TYPE; TYPE OF ACCOUNT (0-COD, 1-CASH, 2-MARGIN, 3-SHORT, 4-SPEC. SUBSCRIPTION, 5-CONV. BOND, 6-SPEC. BOND); SPLIT SHARES; DISCRETIONARY NYSE RULE 408; EMPLOYEE; A.E. NO.; MGR'S. APPROVAL

8 CXL'S ONLY; REF; ORIG STATION; MESSAGE NO.; CUSTOMER NAME

9 COM; A.E. OVERRIDE [R/___]; NEG. ¢ PER SH [M/90 ___]; NEG. DISC. [CD__%]; ST INS OVERRIDE [I/_]

10 COM; SPECIAL DESCRIPTIVE INST. [D/______________________________]; D/UNSOL

11 COM

12 COM

13 CONFIRM LINE CFN LINE 2 & 5

ORDER COPY

the purchase price. If he has to buy in the security at a higher price, he has a loss, of course.

3 . The *number of shares* indicated by numerals; for example, 100, 200, and so on. The order can be a combination of a round lot and an odd lot, say, 250 shares.

4 . The *name of the security.* The security's name may be written out, or abbreviated, or shown by its symbol. Securities listed for trading on a stock exchange are assigned symbols. Also, securities traded only in the OTC market use symbols.

It is not necessary to indicate that the security involved is *common stock.* However, if a company has, say, Class A and Class B common stock, you must indicate which on the order form. Also, the term preferred stock must be indicated. If a company has outstanding more than one kind of preferred stock—for example, 4% preferred and 5% preferred—the order form must show which preferred is intended.

If the order is to buy or to sell bonds, the order form should specify the interest rate and maturity date of the bond.

5 . Whether the order is a *market* order or a *limit* order or a *stop* order. These terms are explained later in this chapter.

6 . The customer's name or code number, and the date the order is entered.

KINDS OF ORDERS

Market Orders

The most common type of order is the *market order,* which instructs you to accept the current market price, that is, the current bid and offer, or quote. If the customer is willing to *buy at the market,* he is willing to accept the lowest offer, whatever it is at that time. If he is willing to *sell at the market,* he is willing to accept the highest bid for his stock. Unless the customer gives you instructions to the contrary, enter his order as a *market* order. Figure 10–2 shows a market order.

Limit Orders

Sometimes a customer is not willing to accept the current market price or is concerned that the market price may move disadvantageously before the order can be executed. For self-protection, the customer can enter a *limit* order (see Figure 10–3), which places a limit on the price that he is willing to pay or receive. With a limit order (also known as a *limited price order*), a customer acquiring securities can never pay more than the limit price on the order, and a customer selling securities can never receive less than the limit.

Figure 10–2. A Market Order

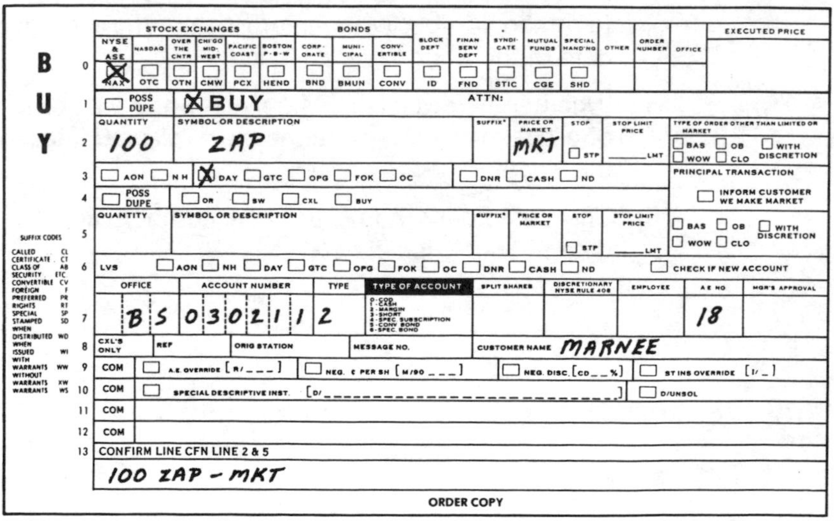
B U Y
STOCK EXCHANGES BONDS EXECUTED PRICE
NYSE & ASE NAX OTC OTN CMW PCX HEND BND BMUN CONV ID FND STIC CGE SHD
POSS DUPE ☒ BUY ATTN:
QUANTITY 100 SYMBOL OR DESCRIPTION ZAP PRICE OR MARKET MKT
AON NH ☒ DAY GTC OPG FOK OC DNR CASH ND
PRINCIPAL TRANSACTION
INFORM CUSTOMER WE MAKE MARKET
OFFICE BS ACCOUNT NUMBER 030211 TYPE 2 TYPE OF ACCOUNT A.E. NO. 18
CUSTOMER NAME MARNEE
COM
CONFIRM LINE CFN LINE 2 & 5
100 ZAP - MKT
ORDER COPY

Normally, a limit order will not be executed immediately. Thus, the customer may specify that the limit order is "good for the day" or "good til cancelled."

Stop Orders

Another kind of order that can be entered is a *stop,* or *stop loss,* order (see Figure 10–4). This is a protection order used to limit loss exposure. It is a memorandum order because it remains dormant until its price is reached or passed, at which time it becomes a market order and is executed. Stop orders are entered "in the money side" of the market and would normally be executed if the "stop instructions" weren't there. For example, Customer A purchases 100 XYZ at 50 for $5,000. If XYZ falls in value, Customer A loses $100 for every point. The most Customer A wants to risk on this transaction is $500. Customer A would instruct his registered representative to enter an order

Figure 10–3. A Limit Order

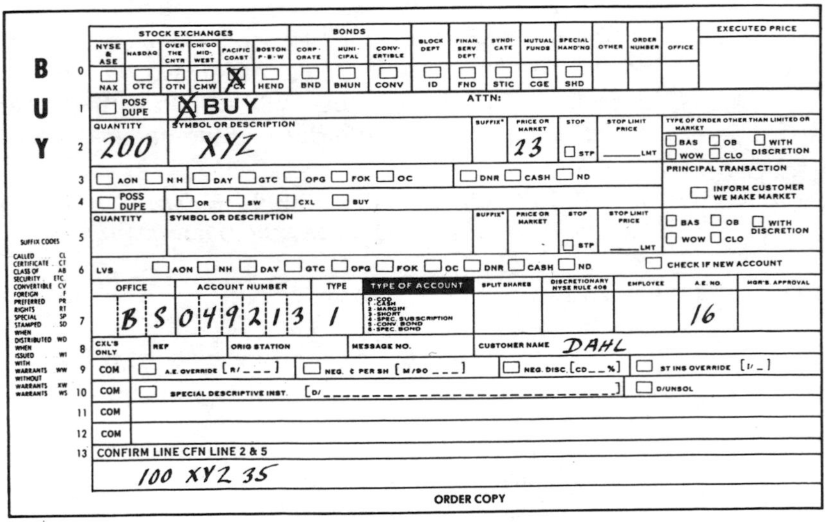
BUY

0 STOCK EXCHANGES: NYSE & ASE NAX; NASDAQ OTC; OVER THE CNTR OTN; CHI'GO MID-WEST CMW; PACIFIC COAST PCX [X]; BOSTON P-B-W HEND
BONDS: CORPORATE BND; MUNICIPAL BMUN; CONVERTIBLE CONV
BLOCK DEPT ID; FINAN SERV DEPT FND; SYNDICATE STIC; MUTUAL FUNDS CGE; SPECIAL HAND'NG SHD; OTHER; ORDER NUMBER; OFFICE; EXECUTED PRICE

1 POSS DUPE; [X] BUY; ATTN:

2 QUANTITY 200; SYMBOL OR DESCRIPTION XYZ; SUFFIX*; PRICE OR MARKET 23; STOP STP; STOP LIMIT PRICE ____LMT; TYPE OF ORDER OTHER THAN LIMITED OR MARKET: BAS, OB, WITH DISCRETION, WOW, CLO

3 AON, N H, DAY, GTC, OPG, FOK, OC, DNR, CASH, ND; PRINCIPAL TRANSACTION

4 POSS DUPE, OR, SW, CXL, BUY; INFORM CUSTOMER WE MAKE MARKET

5 QUANTITY; SYMBOL OR DESCRIPTION; SUFFIX*; PRICE OR MARKET; STOP STP; STOP LIMIT PRICE ____LMT; BAS, OB, WITH DISCRETION, WOW, CLO

6 LVS, AON, NH, DAY, GTC, OPG, FOK, OC, DNR, CASH, ND; CHECK IF NEW ACCOUNT

7 OFFICE BS; ACCOUNT NUMBER 049213; TYPE 1; TYPE OF ACCOUNT: 0-COD, 1-CASH, 2-MARGIN, 3-SHORT, 4-SPEC. SUBSCRIPTION, 5-CONV. BOND, 6-SPEC. BOND; SPLIT SHARES; DISCRETIONARY NYSE RULE 408; EMPLOYEE; A.E. NO. 16; MGR'S. APPROVAL

8 CXL'S ONLY; REF; ORIG STATION; MESSAGE NO.; CUSTOMER NAME DAHL

9 COM; A.E. OVERRIDE [R/___]; NEG. ¢ PER SH [M/90 ___]; NEG. DISC. [CD__%]; ST INS OVERRIDE [I/_]

10 COM; SPECIAL DESCRIPTIVE INST. [D/________________]; D/UNSOL

11 COM

12 COM

13 CONFIRM LINE CFN LINE 2 & 5

100 XYZ 35

ORDER COPY

SUFFIX CODES: CALLED CL; CERTIFICATE CT; CLASS OF SECURITY AB ETC.; CONVERTIBLE CV; FOREIGN F; PREFERRED PR; RIGHTS RT; SPECIAL SP; STAMPED SD; WHEN DISTRIBUTED WD; WHEN ISSUED WI; WITH WARRANTS WW; WITHOUT WARRANTS XW; WARRANTS WS

Figure 10–4. A Stop Order

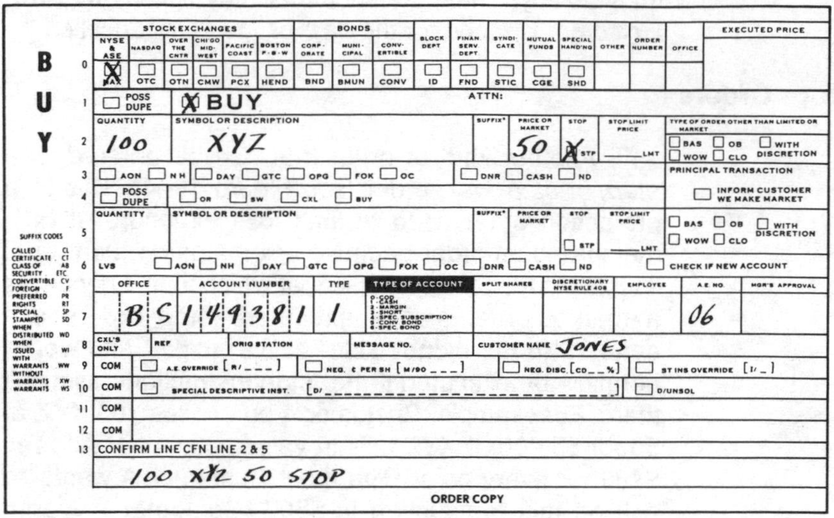

to "sell 100 XYZ @ 45 stop." So long as the security did not trade down to 45, A's order would not be executed. Once it did trade at 45 or below, the order would become a market order and the security would be sold.

A *buy stop order* is entered above the current market. A *sell stop order* is entered below it.

Other Kinds of Orders

Other orders are entered for special purposes. Let's just take a quick look at each so that you will have some familiarity with them:

1. *Stop Limit:* This is the same as stop order, but it becomes a limit order instead of a market order when the stop price is reached.

2. *Fill-or-Kill (FOK):* This order must be executed in its entirely immediately or it's canceled.

3. *Immediate or Cancel (IOC):* Any part of the order may be executed immediately and the rest canceled.

4. *All-or-None (AON):* Given time constraints, such as a day, *all* of the order must be filled or the client does not have to accept the execution.

5. *Spread Order:* Used in listed options and futures trading, a spread order contains the instruction to buy one product or issue and simultaneously sell the same with different terms. For example, "B (buy) 1 call ZAP Apr 40, S (sell) 1 call ZAP Apr 45."

6. *Straddle Order:* Used in listed options, this is the simultaneous purchase or sale of a put and a call on the same underlying stock in the same series. For example, "B (buy) 1 call WIP Jul 60, B (buy) 1 put WIP Jul 60." Straddle orders also apply to certain futures transactions.

7. *Combination Order:* This order is similar to a straddle, but it uses a different series designation.

8. *One Cancels Other (OCO):* This order has two possible executions. The first one to get executed automatically cancels the other. Hence its name: one cancels other.

SHORT SALES

Short sales are sales of securities that the seller does not own. The seller enters a sell order, which the brokerage firm executes. The seller's firm then borrows stock, either from another client's account or from another firm, to make delivery on the sale. The seller is now said to be *short* the stock.

Short sales are a strategy used when the seller expects the value of the security to decrease in the future. The short seller expects to buy the security in the open market at a lower price than that received in the short sale. The seller then turns the securities over to the firm, thereby *covering* the short position. The brokerage firm returns the securities to the client's account or to the lending firm. The difference between the short sale price and the open market purchase price is intended to represent a profit to the short seller.

The short seller pays interest on the borrowed stock as long as the position is open.

PROCESSING THE ORDER

After the order has been written out, the next step is to determine whether the security involved is a *listed* security or an *unlisted* security.

Thousands of securities are traded on the stock exchanges and in the OTC market. It is not possible for a person to remember in which market each security is traded. However, every firm has available various charts and books containing that information.

If the order is for a security listed on an exchange, say, the New York Stock Exchange, it is transmitted to the firm's telephone clerk on the floor of that exchange. The clerk is told whether it is a *buy* or *sell* order, the number of shares, the name of the stock, and the kind of order it is. If it is a *limit* or a *stop* order, then the clerk must also be given the limit or stop price. If it is any other kind of order that has special terms, then these terms, too, must be given to the floor broker. The telephone clerk gives this information to the firm's floor broker, who then tries to execute the order.

Exchange Systems

Several of the exchanges have order and report routing systems that expedite the flow of orders to and from the exchange floor. Firms that partake have their computers "talking" to the exchange's computers, thereby bypassing many of the manual handling steps necessary for nonsystematized orders. Among these systems are the American Stock Exchange's AMOS (Amex Option System) and PERS (Post Execution Reporting System) and the Chicago Board Option

Exchange's RAES (Report Automated Execution System).

On the New York Stock Exchange, orders can be executed by means of the Designated Order Turnaround (DOT) system. If the DOT system is used, the order is sent electronically to the trading post, where the stock is traded. After execution, the order is reported by computer directly to the originating office.

Some of these systems not only route orders, but execute market orders against the current quote automatically. In addition, the identification of executing floor brokers to the trade are captured, along with the firm that they are representing. These data are sent directly to a clearing corporation's comparison systems, obviating the need for the firm to process these transactions through its comparison system later on in the cycle.

Whether or not the firm's order-routing process is systematized, the orders are the order room's responsibility.

Over-the-Counter Executions

If the order is for an OTC security, it is sent to the trading department. The *trader* gets in touch with the broker-dealers who are making a market in that security. The trader will execute the order with the broker-dealer who offers the best price.

At this point, it should be mentioned that each order is time-stamped when it is received and when it is transmitted to the telephone clerk on the floor of the exchange or to the trader in the trading department.

The order is also time-stamped when the telephone clerk or the trader calls back and reports the execution of the order. Time-stamping the order is very important. The information may be needed to settle a dispute as to the price at which the order was executed.

HOW ORDERS ARE EXECUTED

Earlier, you learned how an order is executed on the floor of an exchange and also how an order is executed on the over-the-counter market. So that you may refresh your memory, here's a description of what takes place.

Executing an Order on an Exchange

Let's assume that an order to buy 100 shares of ABC common, at the market, has been transmitted to your firm's telephone clerk on the floor of the exchange. The telephone clerk puts the information on an order slip and sends it out to your firm's floor broker.

When the floor broker receives the slip, he goes to the post at which ABC common is traded. There he gets the latest quote for this stock. Let's assume it's "$35\frac{1}{4}$–$35\frac{3}{4}$."

Your firm's floor broker then calls out his bid "$35\frac{1}{2}$ for 100." This means he is ready to buy 100 shares of ABC common at $35.50 a share.

A floor broker for another firm has an order to sell 100 shares of ABC common, also at the market. He hears the bid and decides to sell at that price. This floor broker then calls out "sold." This means that he is willing to sell 100 shares of ABC common to your floor broker at $35.50 a share.

Your firm's broker now writes the price of "$35\frac{1}{2}$" and the other broker's number on his order slip. He sends the order slip back to your firm's telephone clerk.

You will recall that an order form has been written but that it has no price on it. When the telephone clerk receives the order slip, he reports the execution of the order and gives the price at which it was executed. This price is entered on the order form and a circle is put around it. The reason for circling the price is to show that it is an executed order.

Executing an Order on the OTC Market

Now let's assume that XYZ common is traded on the OTC market. When the registered representative receives the order, he sends it to the order room. There a clerk sends the order to the firm's trading department.

In the trading department, the order is given to a *trader.* The trader contacts several broker-dealers who make a market in XYZ common stock. Usually, a trader calls three broker-dealers. He asks each of them for a quotation. The trader completes the trade with the broker-dealer who gives him the lowest offer.

The trader now enters the price on the order form, together with the broker-dealer's name, and sends it to the order room. The order room reports the execution to the registered representative who took the order.

11   The Purchase and Sales Department

The execution of an order marks the start of a long line of jobs that have to be performed in the operations division of a securities house. Among them are preparing the customer's confirmation and comparing the trade with the other securities house involved. These jobs are done in the purchase and sales (P&S) department. Let us see how these jobs are performed.

Most securities houses now use computers to do much of the work in the purchase and sales department. In other securities houses, clerks still perform all functions by hand. Whether the job is done by a computer or by a clerk, the procedures are almost the same. If the work is done by a computer, the computer is programmed to perform the work that would otherwise be done manually. So, for learning purposes, we shall assume that all functions are performed by hand.

The P&S department is responsible for basically four tasks:

1. Recording.

2 . Figuration.

3 . Comparison and reconcilement.

4 . Confirmation and booking.

RECORDING

To keep track of the huge number of trades each day, each transaction has to be coded. Each trade is assigned a CUSIP, or in-house, number. This number identifies the issuer and issue. In addition, to handle the clearing of a great many trades, known as *tickets,* each is assigned a *code.* The code gives the type of transaction, point of execution, and many other details needed for properly processing the ticket.

FIGURATION

Every trade must undergo a series of computations. How much money was involved in the transaction? How much does the selling firm receive? How much does the buying firm pay? How much does the customer pay or receive? These computations are known as *figuration,* and they are performed by the P&S department.

A trade involves several computations before the amount the customer owes (for a buy) or is owed (for a sell) is known.

1 . The first step in this process is quantity times price:

To illustrate: 100 shares at $42 = $4,200; 1,000 bonds at $94\frac{1}{4}$ = $942.50.

2 . Next, trades involving bonds and other forms of debt instrument carry *accrued interest.* Bonds, for example, pay interest owed every six months. When trade occurs between interest payment dates, the buyer must pay the seller the interest

that has accumulated up to but not including the transaction's settlement date.

Debt instruments pay interest on a predetermined basis. Most bonds, for example, pay their instruments on a semiannual basis. Their description therefore carries two letters that represent the interest payment period:

JJ	—	January & July
FA	—	February & August
MS	—	March & September
AO	—	April & October
MN	—	May & November
JD	—	June & December

To illustrate: A "JJ" bond pays its interest every January 1 and July 1. As corporate bonds use a 360-day year as a basis to compute interest, each month has 30 days. A trade in a J&J corporate bond, settling on February 16, would carry 45-day accrued interest (January 30 + February 15 = 45 days). The buyer would pay the seller 45 days' accrued interest. This money is added to the transaction's computation (quantity x price) and represents the settlement money between transacting firms.

When bonds trade, the buyer must usually pay the seller accrued interest—in addition to the purchase or sale price. Accrued interest is the interest that the buyer must pay the seller in compensation for the time the seller owned the bond since the last interest payment date.

To illustrate: Consider a regular way trade of 10 XYZ, Inc–FA–10% of '99 bonds at $96\frac{3}{8}$ on April 5. The total proceeds that the buyer has to pay the seller is equal to the trade price *plus* the accrued interest. The purchase price is equal to $96\frac{3}{8}$ or $963.75 per bond. Since the trade is for 10 bonds, the trade price is $9,637.50.

You must calculate the accrued interest, which takes two steps. The first step is to determine the number of days that the seller has owned the bond from the last payment date. Interest accrues to the seller until *the day before* the trade settles (*regardless* of which settlement option is used). For corporate bonds, the convention is to assume that each whole month has *30 days* regardless of the actual number of days in the month. Since each month is assumed to have 30 days, then each year must contain 360 days (12 months x 30 days per month).

Thus, if the trade was made on April 5 with a regular way settlement, it settles on April 12, five *business* days after the trade date. The number of days of accrued interest in April would therefore be 11 days—*up to and including the day before the settlement date.*

*April**

S	M	T	W	T	F	S
					1	**2**
3	**4**	**5**	6	7	8	9
10	**11**	12	13	14	15	16
17	18	19	20	21	22	23
24	25	26	27	28	29	30

*Boldface days are accrued days.

Since the bond last paid interest on February 1, the seller is also entitled to receive interest for the entire month of February and the entire month of March (30 days for each month by convention), in addition to 11 days accrued in April, for a total of 71 days accrued.

The second step is to solve this equation:

Accrued interest = Principal x Rate x Time

The *principal* is $10,000 because the trade is for 10 bonds. (Note that the purchase price makes no difference.) The *rate* is the bond's coupon yield expressed as a decimal. The *time* is equal to the number of days accrued divided by 360.

The formula for accrued interest for this bond therefore becomes:

Accrued interest = $10,000 x 0.10 x (71/360) = $197.22

So the total number of dollars due to the seller from the buyer for this trade is:

Purchase price	$9,637.50
Accrued interest	197.22
	$9,834.72

Let's now look at a more unusual example.

To Illustrate: Consider a next-day settlement trade of 20 XYZ, Inc MS–15 8% bonds at a price of $61\frac{1}{8}$ with a July 3 trade date. The purchase price is equal to 20 times $611.25 or $12,225. The formula for calculating the accrued is:

Accrued interest = Principal x Rate x Time
= $20,000 x 0.08 x T

The value of T is equal to the number of days over which interest accrues divided by 360.

On the following calendar, the trade settles on July 7. The day after the trade, July 4, is a legal holiday, and the fifth and sixth are weekend days. So the next business day is the seventh, and the trade settles on that day. Therefore, in July there will be 6 days accrued.

July

S	M	T	W	T	F	S
		1	2	3	4	5
6	7	8	9	10	11	12
13	14	15	16	17	18	19
20	21	22	23	24	25	26
27	28	29	30	31		

Since the last interest payment is on March 15, we now have to compute the number of days from March 15 to July 6.

Month of March (starting on March 15)	16 days
Month of April	30 days
Month of May	30 days
Month of June	30 days
Month of July	6 days
	112 days

So the accrued interest calculation becomes:

Accrued interest = $20,000 x 0.08 x (112/360) = $497.78

and the total dollars due the seller on settlement day become:

$12,225.00 + $497.78 = $12,722.78

While almost all bonds trade with accrued interest, bonds that are in default or income bonds that are not currently paying interest will trade *flat,* that is, without accrued interest. If a bond is trading flat, the seller must disclose that fact to the buyer before the trade is consummated.

3. The next step in the process depends on whether the firm acted as agent or as principal.

Agency transactions carry commission. After May 1, 1975, fixed commission schedules known as "minimum commission" ceased to exist. This "fixed" rate was charged by all firms who were members of the New York Stock Exchange. After "Mayday," firms began to charge different rates from each other as they competed for business, and as a result, each firm now maintains its own commission rate schedule.

Most firms, in setting their rates, allow for discounts based on certain criteria established by the firm's management. In these firms, account executives, in negotiating rates with their clients, must stay within the firm's guidelines. Discounts negotiated between the account executive and the client are usually shared by the firm and account executive.

On purchase transactions, commission is added to the trade money. On sell transactions, commission is subtracted from trade money.

To Illustrate: Customer C.B. Craig Buys 100 shares of Park Ave Ltd at 50 and Sells 100 shares of Skyhawk Airlines at 45. Assume a commission of $50 per transaction.

	First Money	Commission	Net Money
B 100 PAL at 50 =	$5,000 +	$50.00	= $5,050.00
S 100 SAC at 45 =	$4,500 −	$50.00	= $4,450.00

On the purchase, C.B. Craig would owe $5,050. The proceeds of the sell would bring him $4,450.

On *principal transactions,* the firm charges a markup (on a buy order) or a markdown (on a sell order). The charge is imposed by the firm and must be in accordance with NASD's (National Association of Security Dealers) 5% markup guideline.

To Illustrate: Customer Jill Randis Buys 100 shares of Marnee Corp at 30 and Sells 100 shares of Sulton First National Bank and Trust at 45. The firm acts as principal; in other words, Randis bought Marnee Corp from the firm and sold Sulton Bank to the firm. If the firm is charging a $50 markup (down) per transaction, the customer would be billed:

B 100 MARC at $30\frac{1}{2}$ = $3030
S 100 SFNB at $44\frac{1}{2}$ = $4450

As these are not agency transactions, no commission may be charged. Instead, the transactions price has been adjusted to reflect the charge.

4. The last step in figuration is to impose the SEC fee. This charge is imposed on the sale of equity transactions occurring on a national exchange. The fee is .01¢ every $300 of contracted value or fraction thereof.

With figuration completed, the next two cycles begin: comparison and confirmation.

COMPARISON AND RECONCILEMENT

Trades executed on the various exchanges or in the over-the-counter marketplace on behalf of a firm's customer are transacted by verbal agreement between executing participants or *principals.* On the exchanges, these participants are known as floor *brokers;* in the over-the-counter arena, they are known as *traders.* Because no written agreement changes hands at the time of the trade, trade verification or comparison is performed later in the operation cycle.

The reconciliation of the customer transactions to the brokerage firms that were traded with is the most important function performed by the P&S department. For every customer-side transaction, there must be an opposing broker-side transaction.

The process of verifying the firm's own records of a customer's trade is known as *reconcilement.* The process of reconciling the firm's records with those of the opposing broker's records is known as *comparison.* The customer's firm is also known as the broker-side firm, the buying firm, or the executing firm (broker). The broker with which the customer's firm traded is known as the street-side broker, the offsetting broker, the opposing broker, or the *contra* broker (firm).

Every transaction involves two critical dates. The date of execution is known as the *trade date.* The day when delivery and payment is expected is known as the *settlement date.* Listed and most over-the-counter transactions involve a five-day settlement; that is, a trade effected on a Monday is settled five business days later, or on the following Monday.

How Executed Trades Are Compared

Comparison can be made in a couple of ways:

- Firm to firm.
- By means of a contract sheet through the clearing house.

Firm-to-Firm or Broker-to-Broker Comparison

Firm-to-firm comparison requires each firm that was a party to the trade to send a comparison (a written or computer-produced document giving the details of the transaction) to a contra, or opposing, firm. In other words, if a brokerage firm executes 100 trades with 100 firms, the firm sends 100 comparisons, one to each firm. In the same fashion, each of the contra firms sends a trade comparison to each firm that it traded with—and so on. Fortunately, the industry does not process all its trade comparisons through this method.

The Clearing House

The greatest quantity of transactions are compared through a clearing house. The participants submit their trade data to one central location. With all these data collected, the clearing house performs a comparison. It matches buyers with their stated sellers and sellers with their stated buyers. Those transactions in which the buyer and seller agree are reported to the submitting firms as *compared*. If a submitting firm's data do not agree with an opposing firm data, it is reported as *uncompared*. Finally, if an opposing firm submitted data that do not compare with the named firm's data, the data are reported to the named firm as an *advisory*.

The comparison process varies from product to product. Most products are compared through a clearing corporation, or house. A clearing house offers a computerized comparison facility to which the participating firms send their trade data. The system matches the data and produces a series of *contract sheets,* which are listings of the trade information from both the buying firm and the selling firm.

Typical trade data input to a clearing corporation contains the following information:

1. Trade date and settlement date.
2. Clearing house ID number of the submitting firm.
3. Whether the trade was a buy or sell transaction.
4. Quantity of shares.
5. Security description and/or security ID number (CUSIP).
6. Price and settlement amounts.
7. Clearing house ID number of the opposing firm.

These data are passed through a comparison routine that verifies the buyer's definition of the trade against the seller's to find a "match." The data that do match are said to be *compared.* The data that do not match are divided into two categories:

1. Unmatched trades in which the data originated with the submitter (buyer).
2. Unmatched trades in which the data were entered by the contra firm.

The results are printed on the contract sheets.

Contract sheets (see Figure 11–1) are divided into three sections:

- Compared: Submitting firm and contra firm agree to the terms of the trade.
- Uncompared: The contra firm does not agree to the submitting firm's terms.
- Advisory: The contra firm "does not know"—that is, does not recognize—the trade data on the contract.

Figure 11–1. The Regular Way Contract

									CLEARING MEMBER		CM. NO.	TRADE DATE			PURCHASE CONTRACT		SETTL. DATE			National Securities Clearing Corporation

STONE, FORREST & RIVERS — CM. NO. 035 — TRADE DATE MO 04 DAY 04 YR 8X — PURCHASE CONTRACT REGULAR WAY — SETTL. DATE MO 04 DAY 11 YR 8X — SCC-NYSE

COMPARED PURCHASES

SELLER	ACCT OF	QUANTITY	CONTRACT AMOUNT	SUMM DIFF	UNIT PRICE	SPEC CODE	ADJ CODE	SELLER	ACCT OF	QUANTITY	CONTRACT AMOUNT	SELLER	ACCT OF	QUANTITY	CONTRACT AMOUNT	CONTROL NO.
CNS	AJB	AMERICAN JELLY BEAN CUSIP: 0C3456106		000												
	164	100	3,800.00		38.00000											0213892
	TOTAL	100	3,800.00													
CNS	POW	POWER COMPANY CUSIP: 642311105		000												
	590	100	1,600.00		16.00000											02364137
	TOTAL	100	1,600.00													
					15.87500			590		100	1,587.50					01247231
					15.62500							590		100	1,562.50	02436483
CNS	RAM	RAMS SHOE INC. CUSIP: 723103103		000	24.00000							336		100	2,400.00	0213746
CNS	SOP	SWAMP OPTICAL LTD. CUSIP: 734026104		000												
	031	100	5,450.00		54.50000											02940341
	TOTAL	100	5,450.00													
CNS	ZAP	ZAPPETCH CORP CUSIP: 829462107		000	32.12500			305		100	3,212.50					04983411

UNCOMPARED PURCHASES / **ADVISORY DATA**

SUBJECT TO THE BY-LAWS AND THE RULES OF NSCC
SCL 10

ODD PENNY BREAKAGE — APPROXIMATE DECIMAL EQUIVALENT

ADJUSTMENT CODES
A1 ADDED BY ADVISORY
A2 SUPPLEMENTAL ADD BY SELLER
*DESIGNATES TRANSACTION OUT OF HI-LO PRICE RANGE.
D3 DELETE CONTRACT COMPARED ITEM OR ADVISORY
D4 DELETE ADD BY SELLER
OL ODD LOT
A7 FAIL ADD BY SELLER
K STOCK FAIL DELETE

B U Y

After the first set of contract reports are received, the P&S personnel begin to research trade differences. If they determine that the contra version of the transaction is correct, they send only certain notices to the clearing corporation advising them that the firm will accept the transaction. These items then become *compared trades* and will appear on subsequent contract sheets as such.

The number of corrective routines depends on the product's settlement cycle (stocks and corporate bonds have two cycles, or corrective routines; options and futures, one). It is also a function of automation. As options and futures transactions are next-day settlers, comparison is affected on the night of trade date. Equity and corporate bonds, as well as municipal bonds, undergo comparison during the five-business-day cycle (from trade date to settlement date), with a corrective cycle being performed on the second and third day.

Transactions that are not compared through a clearing corporation are said to compare *ex-clearing corporation.* In such cases, the buying firm and selling firm complete comparison forms for each trade and submit them to each other. If the receiving firm's personnel agrees to the terms displayed, they will affix the firm's stamp to one copy of the form and return it to the originator. The other copy is retained for their records.

Regardless of the cycle used, there eventually exists transactions that cannot be compared by the P&S personnel. These problem trades are returned to the point of execution for reconcilement by the individuals who participated in the actual trade or execution process.

On the New York Stock Exchange, equity or bond transactions are returned to the broker who executed the order on behalf of the firm's customer. The processes, named after the form used to identify the problem, are known as *questioned trade* (QT) (see Figure 11–2). The same process on the Amex is known as *DKs* (don't know). The Chicago Board

Figure 11–2. A Questioned Options Trade

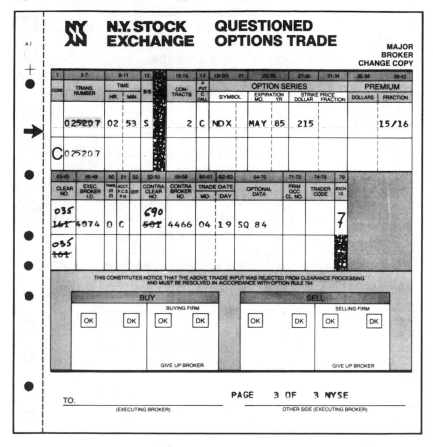

Option Exchange refers to this process as *rejected option trade notices* (ROTNs).

The participants to the trade discuss the events leading to the transaction. If the parties agree, the firm that had been in error signs the correct firm's version of the trade, and this "accepted" transaction then enters the comparison process.

Work of the Clearing Corporation

The clearing corporation makes it possible for brokerage firms to process the great volume of trades that occur daily. To compare a trade through the clearing corporation, participating firms submit the details of their trades to the clearing corporation. These data are processed through the computer system into concise sets of reports, which are used by the brokerage firm's P&S department to reconcile their transactions.

Note: A firm that reports a transaction to its client does not have a true trade until the other side (the street side or contra side) knows (or agrees to) it.

The comparison contract report usually contains three categories of trade data:

- *Compared*—the firm to which the contract sheets are issued submitted trade data that the contra (opposing) firm agrees with.
- *Uncompared*—the firm to which the contract sheets are issued submitted data that the named contra firm does not know.
- *Advisory* (aka *adjustment*)—data that an opposing firm has submitted that the contra firm does not know.

To illustrate: A trade occurs between Stone Forrest & Rivers (SFR) and Giant Recker & Crane (GRC). On Stone Forrest & Rivers' contract sheet:

If the trade is compared, SFR's data agree with GRC's version of the trade.

If the trade is uncompared, SFR's data are unknown to GRC.

If the trade is advisory, SFR does not know GRC's trade data.

In this example, a price difference in the data submitted to the clearing corporation by the buying and selling firms would result in SFR's version of the trade appearing in the uncompared category, while GRC's version would appear in SFR's advisory category.

The P&S function now goes through a corrective process by accepting, when appropriate, the contra firm's version of the trade. This acceptance is submitted to the clearing corporation where it is processed and appears on the next round of contract sheets.

The number of sets of contract reports issued by the clearing corporation or computer facility processing these data depends on the settlement cycle of the transaction. As option trades settle the next business day, two sets of comparison reports are issued on the night of trade date. For stocks that have a five-business-day cycle, three main sets of contract sheets are issued.

The responsibility of a clearing corporation for transactions differs from product to product. In some clearing corporations, their responsibility for the trade begins at trade submission; in others, it begins after comparison.

The primary clearing corporations are:

- Midwest Clearing Corporation (MCC).
- Mortgage Backed Securities Clearing Corporation (a division of MCC)—MBSCC.
- National Securities Clearing Corporation (NSCC).
- Option Clearing Corporation (OCC).
- Pacific Clearing Corporation (PCC).
- Stock Clearing Corporation of Philadelphia (SCCP).

National Security Clearing Corporation issues three main sets of comparison reports for listed equity transactions. They are:

- *Regular way contracts*—produced the night after trade date, or trade date plus 1.
- *Supplemental contracts*—produced the night of trade date plus 2.
- *Added trade contracts*—produced the night of trade date plus 3.

The transactions compared by the processing of the added trade contracts (trade date plus 3) are then processed into the settlement routines.

Netted Balance Orders

For trades to be compared successfully, each purchase must have an offsetting sell transaction. The only possible differences are in the execution prices. The clearing corporation adjusts these price differences by crediting or debiting the money differences between the participating firms. Thus all of the transactions in a given security on a given day reflect the value of one given price.

With this adjustment applied, all of the transactions are homogeneous. It is now possible to net (pair off) each firm's street side purchases against their own sales on a given day.

The result of this netting process would leave only a few "receives" and "deliveries" to be performed among the clearing firms. A firm that purchased more shares than it sold would be netted to a receive position, whereas a firm that sold more shares than it purchased would net to a deliver position. Firms with a net receive position would be issued a *receive balance order* by the clearing corporation against a firm that was a net seller. A firm with a net deliver position would be issued a *deliver balance order* against a firm that was a net buyer.

To Illustrate: Stone Forrest & Rivers (SFR) enters into and compares the following transactions of Hamingson & Hamingson:

B 100 at 43 from GRC
S 100 at $43\frac{1}{8}$ to SVR
B 100 at $43\frac{1}{4}$ from DUN

Dunbar Associates (DUN) participation:

B 100 at 43 from SVR
B 100 at 43 from GRC
S 100 at $43\frac{1}{8}$ to GRC
S 100 at $43\frac{1}{4}$ to SFR

Giant Recker & Crane (GRC) traded:

S 100 at 43 to SFR
S 100 at 43 to DUN
B 100 at $43\frac{1}{8}$ from DUN

Stevar Ltd (SVR):

S 100 at 43 to DUN
B 100 at $43\frac{1}{8}$ from SFR

The first step employed by the clearing corporation is to institute a *settlement price.* The price used in this example will be $43 per share.

SFR has two purchases and one sale
DUN has two purchases and two sales
GRC has one purchase and two sales
SVR has one purchase and one sale

SFR will be issued a receive balance order (RBO) to receive 100 shares from GRC. GRC receives a delivery balance order (DBO) to deliver 100 shares to SFR.

SFR has a customer selling stock for $43\frac{1}{8}$ and another customer buying at $43\frac{1}{4}$. The price difference between these two transactions is $\frac{1}{8}$ of a point or $12.50 ($\frac{1}{8}$ x 100 shares). The buying customer owes

SFR $12.50 more than the firm owes the selling customer. The clearing corporation charges SFR the $12.50.

DUN has two customers selling stock for prices higher than the settlement price and two customers purchasing stock at the settlement price. Therefore, the sellers will be looking for $37.50 more than the buying customers will pay (sales at $43\frac{1}{8}$ and $43\frac{1}{4}$ vs. purchases at 2x43). The clearing corporation will credit DUN the $37.50.

GRC has a customer who purchased stock at $\frac{1}{8}$ of a point higher than the settlement price. That customer will pay the firm, and the clearing corporation will charge the firm $12.50.

Finally, SVR also has a client that purchased stock above the industry-imposed settlement price. The firm will be charged the $\frac{1}{8}$ point ($12.50) by the clearing corporation.

National Securities Clearing Corporation has charged SFR, GRC, and SVR $12.50 each ($12.50 x 3 = $37.50) and credited Dun $37.50. By this adjustment, all price differences intrafirm have been neutralized.

In reality, all securities traded by the firm go through this adjustment process and the results are netted to one cash figure.

Continuous Net Settlement

Before the day of the clearing corporation, if the netted balance orders were settled on their settlement date, the books of that day's transactions could be closed. If they were not, the items would become "fail to receives" or "fail to delivers." As each day's processing cycle passed, the number of fail items would grow.

With the introduction of the depository concept, settlement of transactions could be affected by book entry maintained by the depository. This, in turn, meant that the instructions to receive or deliver vs. transaction settlement could be maintained by the clearing corporation on a master record file. The master file, containing settling buy and sell transactions, could be passed from NSCC's computers to DTC's computers where the settling positions applied to the firm's deposited securities position.

Those transactions that could be settled or "cleaned up" were; those that could not be settled became fail items. However, as trades pending settlement and the firm's settling positions were maintained on central files, fails from one day could be "rolled" into the next day's settling transactions and netted to a single position. This process is known as *continuous net settlement* (CNS).

Under this procedure, netted transactions in a given security of a given firm that are not cleared or "cleaned up" on their settlement date are included with the next day's settling transactions. These entries are then netted to produce a new settlement position. Therefore, in each security cleared through the CNS process, a firm's pending position is comprised of the results of previous unsettled position and new transactions merged into one position. That position can be either a fail to receive, a fail to deliver, or *flat* (zero position).

To illustrate: On settlement date May 5, Stone Forrest & Rivers is a net buyer of 100 shares of Century Products. The security is not received and the item becomes a fail to receive. On settlement date May 6, Stone Forrest & Rivers is a net seller of 100 shares. The open item, the fail to receive of 100 shares, would be added to these settling transactions, netting the position for the firm to zero.

Money Settlement

As each day's trades settle, notification of the book entry movement is reported to the affected firm. The monies involved with these trades are also reported. The clearing corporation accumulates the sums of what the firm owes for settled purchases and what is owed on settled sales, taking into account the adjusted price, to produce one total settlement money figure. The firm either pays or receives one check versus the clearing corporation to settle all their trades that day.

Ex-Clearing Corporation Trades

Trades not compared through a clearing corporation or through the computer facility of a clearing corporation are said to be compared *ex the clearing corporation*. In this form of comparison, buying and selling firms exchange comparison forms directly, and these types of transactions are therefore compared on a *trade-for-trade* basis. The buying firm and selling firm review each other's comparisons. If they agree with the terms of the trade, they stamp the contra firm comparison and return it to the sender. If they do not agree, they enter into a DK (don't know) type of procedure.

In active and heavily traded marketplaces, trade-for-trade comparisons are all but impossible to process. The sheer volume of paper would make the process uncontrollable. Hence the clearing corporation concept.

Reconcilement

Because the trades that Brokerage Firm A is trying to compare with the contra firms were executed on behalf of A's customers, Firm A must not only reconcile broker differences but also customer differences. The net result of this reconcilement is that for every customer transaction, there will be an opposing broker transaction. These transactions must balance as to shares, security, execution price, and trade money.

The P&S department must research each discrepancy and make the appropriate corrective entry. The resolution of the discrepancy may result in an adjustment to be made to the customer transaction or a correction to the firm's broker-side transaction.

Corrections to the customer transaction require that corrective confirmations be sent to the customer as well as that the adjusting entries be processed through the entire operating cycle.

For trades having a five-day settlement cycle, all corrections to the broker-side entries should be effected by the third business day following the trade date. This is necessary to allow the cashiers department sufficient time to prepare for settlement. Any trade not resolved by the P&S department by the morning of the third business day must be returned to the place of execution for reconcilement. Executions in listed securities are sent to the executing floor brokers. Over-the-counter transactions are returned to the firm's traders. These individuals contact the opposing firm's representative with whom they originally traded. Between the two, they resolve the difference.

As stated earlier, not all transactions are compared through a clearing corporation. Those that are not must be compared on a trade-for-trade basis with the opposing brokerage firm. Both firms exchange comparisons ("comps"). If a firm agrees with the details of the opposing firm's "comp," the firm affixes its stamp to it and returns the stamped copy to the sender. The firm's stamp on the opposing firm's comparison is official acceptance of the transaction. If, on the other hand, the firm does not agree to the terms or does not know the trade at all, it marks the opposing firm's trade comparison "DK" for "don't know." Then it returns the "comp" to the originating firm. Each DK'd item must be researched by the sending firm. If it cannot be reconciled by the P&S department, the original transaction is returned to the executing person for reconcilement.

This concludes the discussion of comparison. All transactions between firms must be compared. Comparison cycles differ among the types of security, their marketplace, and their respective settlement cycle. Regardless of these differences, at the end of the comparison cycle, customer's transactions must agree, or balance, with street-, or broker-, side trades.

PREPARING THE
CUSTOMER'S CONFIRMATION

When the registered representative learns that the customer's order has been executed, he notifies the customer. At this point, all the customer is told is that he has bought or sold a specific number of shares of a security at a particular price. He is not given any details about the commission, taxes, or other fees. The customer learns these details from the *customer's confirmation* that is mailed to him by the securities house.

The customer's confirmation may be manually typed or computer-generated. Usually prepared the night the trade is processed, these confirmations are placed in the mail the next morning.

The customer's confirmation is prepared either in the P&S department by a clerk or if the firm has automation, through programs processed by the computer. The computation of the monies involved, commission, and the like is performed beforehand by either manual or automated processes.

The customer's confirmation contains the following information (see Figure 11–3):

1. A description of the trade (bought or sold).
   The quantity.
   The security's name.
   The execution price.
   The settlement money.
   The accrued interest (if applicable).
   The commission (for an agency trade).
   The SEC fee (for a listed equity sale), other fees, or handling charges.
2. The trade date.
3. The settlement date.
4. The place of execution.
5. The capacity in which the firm acted (agency, principal, or principal as market maker).

Figure 11–3. A Typical Confirmation. Reprinted with permission from David M. Weiss, *After the Trade Is Made* (New York: New York Institute of Finance, 1986).

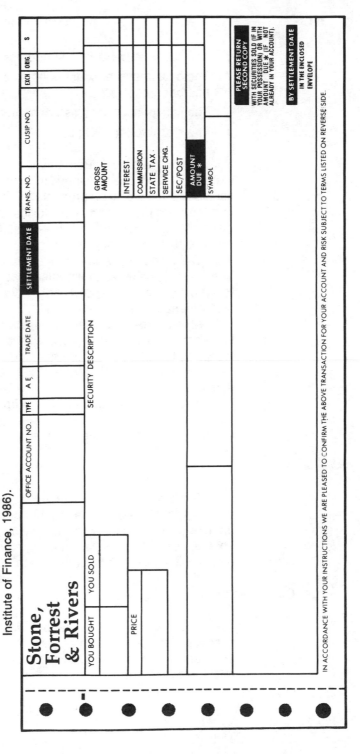

6 . The customer's name and address.

7 . The customer's account number to which the trade has been booked.

8 . The type of account (cash or margin).

9 . The stockbroker's ID number.

Some firms even include the customer settlement instruction and the business phone number of the customer's registered representative. Some brokerage firms use simple confirmation forms; others use fairly elaborate kinds, including a tear-off stub to be returned with the customer's check.

The customer 's confirmation is a multipart form: The original is mailed to the customer; other copies go to the margin department, the bookkeeping department, and the stock record department.

At the same time that the customer's confirmation is prepared, it is usual to prepare a so-called *blotter* or list giving the details of each buy and sell trade for the day. Copies of the blotters are sent to the cashier's department for its use.

Also, the P&S department prepares *exchange* (comparison) tickets. These are used to confirm transactions with the other brokers.

The Amount

The amount (or the execution price) is the price per share multiplied by the number of shares. It shows the cost of the security to the *buying* broker. Stated another way, it is the amount of money the *selling* broker will receive when he delivers the security.

The Commission

The commission is the broker's charge for his services. The commission varies with the dollar amount involved. It is based on the minimum rate schedules adopted by the firm.

The Total, or Net, Amount

On a *buy* order, settlement money is the *amount* plus the *commission.* This total, or net, amount is the *cost* of the security to the customer.

On a *sell* order, the total, or net, amount is the amount less the sum of the commission, transfer taxes, and a registration fee. At present, on sell orders executed in New York, the customer pays a stock transfer tax. The net amount remaining after the commission, taxes, and fees have been deducted is the *net proceeds* to the customer.

The SEC Fee

On all sell orders executed on an organized stock exchange the customer also pays an SEC registration fee. This registration fee is imposed by federal law. It is figured at the rate of .01¢ for each $300 of value, or fraction thereof.

BOOKING

Once the trade has been processed and balanced, it must be entered on the firm's records, or *booked.* Part of the booking procedure is the recording of fees and commissions due to the firm. As always in operations, booking errors can cost the firm money to correct.

12   The Margin
                Department

The responsibility for making sure that clients of the firm maintain their accounts in accordance with rules and regulations is the responsibility of the margin department. These rules and regulations are found in Regulation T of the Federal Reserve and the NYSE maintenance rules. In the control of this department's staff are the money owed to or by the firm, securities owed to or by the firm, and securities owned by the client but retained by the firm.

All customer transactions, including those for cash accounts, pass through the margin department. The margin department performs several highly specialized and important functions: It keeps up-to-date records of each customer's purchase and sale of securities and of each customer's deposit and withdrawal of funds. No money or securities may be paid or delivered to a customer unless authorized by the margin department. In addition, this department keeps records of, and watches carefully, each *margin* transaction in a customer's account. Thus, it makes certain that no violation of the margin rules takes place.

Most securities houses now use computers to do part of the work of the margin department. In a few other securities houses, all the work is still done by hand. However, no matter how the work is performed, the basic procedures and rules we shall study here are the same. So, for our purposes here, we shall assume that all functions are performed by hand.

You will recall that, when a customer opens an account with a securities house, he tells the registered representative the kind of account he wants to open—a *cash* account or a *margin* account.

A *cash* account means just what the name implies: The customer agrees to pay promptly the full price of each security he buys. In a *margin* account, on the other hand, the customer agrees to pay a certain prescribed percentage of the purchase price; the broker lends him the balance of this price.

Generally, when a customer opens an account with a brokerage firm, a notice to that effect is sent to the margin department. The notice shows the customer's name, his account number, and the kind of account (cash or margin) that he has opened. This information is placed on the *customer's account card.*

HANDLING CASH ACCOUNTS

A customer's account report is usually divided into *debit* and *credit* columns.

The *debit* column shows securities purchased by the customer or received for his account. It also shows any monies owed to the brokerage firm. Thus, if the customer owes the firm any money for the purchase of securities, we say he has a *debit* balance.

On the other hand, the *credit* column shows all sales of securities made by the customer or delivered from the account. It also shows any monies deposited or owed from the sale of securities. Thus, if the customer has not been paid the proceeds of a sale or if he elects to keep the money on deposit with the broker, the customer's account has a *credit balance.*

To Illustrate: A customer buys 100 shares of XYZ common. The total amount is $5,000 including commissions. The P&S department prepares a customer's confirmation, showing the details of the transactions. It sends a copy of this confirmation to the margin department, which uses the confirmation to make the entry in the *debit* column.

Because this is a cash account, the customer must pay for the stock in full. When the check is received by the firm, the margin department is notified and an entry is made in the *credit* column.

Following are the rules governing *cash* accounts:

1. When a customer enters an order to purchase a stock, he must have sufficient funds in his account or he must have agreed to make prompt payment in full.

2. If the purchase order is executed, the customer should pay the purchase price in full by the settlement date, but he can pay it not later than the seventh business day after the trade date. In other words, if a customer buys stock on, say, Monday, he should pay for it by the following Monday, but not later than the second following Wednesday. If the customer does not pay for the stock by the seventh business day, then the broker must cancel the trade or liquidate the account. To *liquidate the account* means that the broker sells the security. Under special circumstances, the broker may apply for an extension of time in which the customer can pay for the purchase.

3. When a customer enters an order to sell *long,* the broker must know that the customer owns the security. If the security is not in the broker's possession, the broker must be assured that the customer will deposit it promptly in his account. A *long* sale means that the customer is the owner of the security and that the security is either in his or in his broker's possession.

4. If a customer buys a security and then sells it before paying for it, the account is *restricted.* This means that the broker may not execute new purchase orders for the customer for 90 days, unless the customer deposits enough money in his account to pay for the securities before the new orders are executed. However, the account will not be *restricted* if the customer pays for the purchase within seven business days *and* does not withdraw the proceeds of sale before the payment clears.

   To illustrate: A customer buys 100 XYZ common on Monday, but he does not pay for the stock. On Wednesday of the same week, the customer sells the 100 XYZ common. He asks that the check for the difference be sent to him. This is not permitted.
   Suppose that on this same transaction the customer pays for the shares of stock on Friday. Then, on the following Tuesday, he asks that the check for the sale proceeds be sent to him. This is permitted.

5. A customer may not sell a security *short* in a cash account. Instead, short sales must be made in a *margin account.* A *short* sale means that the customer is selling stock he does not own but that he hopes to buy back at a later date at a lower price. Until such time as the customer buys back the stock, the broker borrows the stock for him from someone else.

HANDLING MARGIN ACCOUNTS

Before we begin our study of *margin* accounts, review the differences between a *cash* account and a *margin* account. Bear in mind that the broker must pay for the stock in full whether the purchase is made in a cash account or in a margin account.

The Margin Agreement

When a customer opens a margin account, he signs an agreement. Among other things, this agreement gives the broker the right to use the securities in the account as collateral for the broker's loans to the customer. This agreement allows the broker to pledge the customer's securities and is called a *hypothecation agreement.*

Remember, when a customer buys on margin, he borrows part of the purchase price from the broker. The broker, in turn, has to borrow the money from a bank. The broker uses the securities in the margin account for collateral.

Basic Terms Used in Margin Accounts

To become a margin clerk, you must have specialized training. Among other things, you must learn the meanings of certain basic terms. We will explain:

1. Current market value.
2. Equity.
3. Credit balance.
4. Debit balance.
5. Loan value.
6. Regulation T (Reg T) excess.
7. Buying power.
8. Minimum maintenance requirement.

Every account can be divided into three parts:

1. *Current market value.* The total of the current market values of all securities maintained in the account.
2. *Equity.* The amount, in either a dollar value or a percentage, of the total current value in the account that belongs to the customer, should the account be liquidated.

3 . *Credit balance.* The amount of money in the account belonging to the customer, or *debit balance*, the amount of money loaned by the firm or owed by the customer.

These components are related by a mathematical formula:

Equity = Current market value – Debit balance

As the current market value fluctuates, so does the customer's *equity.* Not subject to market fluctuations is the *debit balance,* which is the amount loaned by the firm to the customer. Because the customer must repay this debt at a later time, it is therefore an obligation of the customer.

In a cash purchase (when the customer pays for the purchase in full), no debit balance is incurred, and the customer's equity always equals the current market value.

Current Market Value. Generally, the *current market value* (CMV) of a security is the closing price of that security as of the preceding business day. For example, to find the *current market value* of a security on Tuesday, you would take the closing price of that security on Monday. However, there are these exceptions: On the day a security is purchased, its current market value for that day is the total cost of that security, including the commission. And on the day a security is sold, its current market value for that day is the net amount (that is, the amount minus the commission, fees, and taxes).

To Illustrate: On Monday a customer buys on margin 100 shares of XYZ stock at $50 a share. The total cost is $5,044 ($5,000 plus $44 commission). Thus, on Monday, the *current market value* of XYZ stock is $5,044, the total cost of the stock to the customer.

The closing price of XYZ stock on Monday is $52 a share. So its *current market value* on Tuesday is 100 x $52, or $5,200.

Equity. The *equity* (Eq) in an account is the difference between the current market value of the securities in the account and the customer's debit balance. Stated another way, *equity* equals *current market value* minus *debit balance*. It represents the customer's ownership interest in the account.

A customer's equity fluctuates with the market value of the shares in his account. If the market value of the shares rises, his *equity* will be larger. If the market value of his shares decreases, then his *equity* will be smaller.

To illustrate: On April 15, a customer buys on margin 100 shares of XYZ stock for a total cost of $5,000. On the same day, the customer deposits $4,000 with his broker, leaving a *debit balance* of $1,000. The closing price of the stock on April 15 is $52 a share, and on April 16 the closing price is $48 a share. What is the *equity* in the customer's account on April 15, April 16, and April 17?

Answer: On April 15, his *equity* is $4,000. Remember that the current market value of a security on the date of purchase is the total cost of that security. Thus, on April 15, the *current market value* of the security was $5,000. Subtracting $1,000 (the *debit balance*) leaves an equity of $4,000.

However, on April 16, the customer's *equity* is $4,200. Because the closing price of stock on the day before was $52 a share, its *current market value* is now $5,200. Subtracting the *debit balance* of $1,000 leaves an *equity* of $4,200.

But on April 17, the *equity* in the account would be $3,800. The closing price of stock on the day before was $48 a share, so its *current market value* is now $4,800. Subtracting the *debit balance* of $1,000 leaves an *equity* of $3,800.

Credit Balance. The *credit balance* (Cr) is the amount of cash left in a customer's account after he has paid for all his purchases in full. Therefore, a customer's account cannot have a debit and a credit balance at the same time.

To illustrate: A customer deposits $2,000 with the broker at the time he opens his account. The customer then buys 100 shares of XYZ stock, costing $3,000. Several days later he sends the broker a check for $3,000. The $3,000 check is in full payment of the purchase, so the customer still has his initial deposit of $2,000 in his account. This $2,000 is his *credit balance.*

Debit Balance. The *debit balance* (Db) is the amount of money a customer who is buying on margin has borrowed from his broker to finance a purchase. The debit balance will not change because of any increase or decrease in the value of the security so purchased. However, the debit balance will change when the customer makes another margin purchase in his account.

To illustrate: A customer buys on margin 100 shares of XYZ stock worth $6,000. The customer sends the broker a check for $4,800. Thus, he owes the broker $1,200. This $1,200 is his *debit balance.*

Loan Value. The reverse of the margin requirement (discussed later in this chapter) is the *loan value (LV),* which is the amount that the customer may borrow on the security. Together, the margin rate (requirement) and the loan value, both expressed as a percentage, must total 100%. If the Federal Reserve Board establishes a margin rate of 60%, then the loan value of the security is 40%. If the customer is required to pay 70%, then the loan value is 30%.

To illustrate: The margin rate is 60%, so the loan value has to be 40%. A client buys 100 DUD at 50 and deposits the entire amount. Then:

100 XYZ @ 50	$5,000
Less debit balance	0
Customer's equity	$5,000

Reg T Excess. The market value of stocks purchased on margin may rise. When it does, the increased value is known as *excess equity.* It is "excess" because it is more than the equity required by Regulation T, or Reg T, of the Federal Reserve Board. *Reg T* is discussed in detail later in this chapter.

To Illustrate: Assuming a margin rate of 60%, a customer buys 100 shares of DUD at 50. The client deposits $3,000 (60%) and borrows $2,000 (40%).

Equity + Loan value   = Market value
$3,000 + $2,000   = $5,000

The market value of DUD increases to $100 per share and so the current market value of the 100 shares in the account is $10,000 ($100 x 100 shares). Since the customer borrows only $2,000 for the original purchase, the equity is $8,000.

Margin rate + Loan value   = Market value
$6,000 + $4,000   = $10,000
Margin value − Debit   = $10,000 − $2,000
$10,000 − $2,000   = $8,000 (Equity)

The client calls his registered representative and asks if any more money can be borrowed. The rep relays the question to the margin department, where an employee performs the following computation:

Current market value	$10,000
Times the loan value (40%)	0.40
Loan value ($)	$ 4,000
Less debit balance (amount borrowed)	$ 2,000
Reg T excess	$ 2,000

The client may withdraw the $2,000 Reg T excess as cash.

Buying Power. Anytime the loan value is greater than the debit balance in the account, the difference is *excess,* which can be used to calculate *buying power.* A client may apply Reg T excess in an account to a margin purchase. The excess equity is then said to have *buying power.* It represents the part of the purchase price that the client can use instead of cash.

What, then, is the maximum purchase that the client can make on margin? To arrive at that amount, simply divide margin rate into the buying power dollar amount.

To illustrate: The $2,000 excess can be applied by the client to a new trade. The excess equals 60% of what can be bought.

$$\text{Buying power} = \frac{\text{Reg T excess}}{\text{Margin rate}}$$

$$= \frac{\$2,000}{0.60} = \$3,333.33$$

In other words, the current market value of any new purchase can be up to $3,333.34 without the client having to deposit more equity. Of that total value, $2,000 (60%) is equity applied from the client's excess equity, and $1,333.34 (40%) is a new loan from the brokerage firm. The client decides to buy $3,333.34 worth of ROS. The client can purchase $3,333.34 worth of marginable securities.

Current market value	$13,333.34
DUD $10,000.00	
ROS 3,333.34	
Less equity	<u>8,000.00</u>
DUD $ 6,000	
ROS 2,000	
Debit balance	<u>$5,333.34</u>

The client has substituted excess loan value ($2,000) with securities. The debit balance of $5,333.34 is the equivalent of the loan value of 40%

($13,333.34 x 0.40). The equity of $8,000 is the equivalent of the margin rate ($13,333.34 x 0.60).

Note: Minimum maintenance requirements are discussed in the next section.

REGULATION OF MARGIN ACCOUNTS

Transactions in a *margin* account are governed by the rules of the Federal Reserve Board, the rules of the stock exchange on which the security is traded, and the rules of the firm handling the account. As a margin clerk, it is your job to see that none of these rules are broken. A violation of the Federal Reserve rules or, say, the New York Stock Exchange rules could mean that penalties would be imposed on your firm.

Regulation T (Reg T)

The backbone of all margin rules is a Federal Reserve Board regulation known as *Regulation T.* The Federal Reserve Board writes and changes Regulation T. The NYSE and the NASD enforce it.

One of Reg T's provisions stipulates the percentage of margin (that is, the amount that the customer must put into the account), which is known as the *margin rate* (also known as the *initial margin requirement*). The rate is determined by the Federal Reserve Board.

Initial Margin Requirements

The *initial margin* is the amount of money that a customer must deposit with his broker when he buys a security on margin. Both the Federal Reserve Board and the various exchanges have rules on initial margins.

Minimum Equity

The Federal Reserve Board's rule is a *minimum* equity requirement. This states that a firm cannot lend a client money if the client's equity is below $2,000.

To illustrate: A customer opens a margin account and buys 100 shares of XYZ stock on margin at a total cost of $2,000. How much money must he deposit with the broker?
Answer: $2,000. If the margin rate is 50% and the client purchases $3,000 worth of stock as an opening transaction, the margin calculation is $1,500. But the minimum requirement of $2,000 then goes into effect.
If the margin rate is 50% and the client purchases $5,000 worth of stock, what is the requirement?
Answer: $2,500.

In addition to the rules of the Federal Reserve Board and those of the various exchanges, each brokerage firm normally has its own margin rules. These rules cannot be less stringent than those of the exchange of which the firm is a member. For example, a brokerage firm's rules could not permit a customer to make a deposit of, say, $1,800, when the stock exchange requires a deposit of $2,000. However, a brokerage firm could require that a customer make a deposit of more than $2,000.

Time for Deposit of Margin

The rules also specify the time within which a margin customer must deposit the necessary funds with the broker. At present, the rules state that a customer who buys on margin must deposit the required amount within five business days after the transaction.

To illustrate: If a customer buys a security on margin on a Monday, he would have to deposit the required amount by the following Monday. However, under the rules, if there are exceptional circumstances, the broker may ask for an extension of time.

It is the job of the margin clerk to see that the necessary deposits are made on time. He keeps track of this through the customer's account card. You may recall that when the customer buys stock, the date is noted on his account card. If the margin clerk finds that the customer has not made the necessary deposit, he will notify his department head. Under the rules, the brokerage firm must liquidate the purchase if the deposit is not made on time.

Minimum Maintenance Requirements

In addition to the *initial* margin requirements, the New York Stock Exchange also has what it calls *minimum maintenance* requirements. These requirements spell out the amount of equity the customer must have in his margin account after he has bought the securities. The purpose of these requirements is to protect the brokerage firm against any losses should the price of the security go down.

Under the New York Stock Exchange maintenance rules, a customer who has a *long* position in securities must maintain an equity of 25% of the market value of these securities. Thus, if a customer has securities with a current market value of $10,000 in a margin account, his equity would have to be at least $2,500 (25% of $10,000).

To illustrate: A customer has a *debit balance* of $2,500 in his margin account. The *current market value* of the securities in this account is $8,000. Thus, the *equity* in his account is $5,500 ($8,000 − $2,500).

In the foregoing example, the account would meet the *minimum maintenance requirements* of the New York Stock Exchange. *Reason:* Under this requirement, the customer must have an equity of $2,000 (25% of $8,000). His actual equity is $5,500, which is greater than the $2,000 minimum. However, should the price of the securities drop sharply, then the customer's account may not meet the maintenance requirement.

To Illustrate: A customer has a *debit balance* of $2,500 in his margin account. The *current market value* of the securities is now $3,000. Thus, his *equity* in the account is $500 ($3,000 − $2,500). However, under the NYSE rule, his equity in the account must be at least $750 (25% of $3,000). Because the equity ($500) is less than the maintenance requirement ($750), the account is undermargined.

An account becomes *undermargined* when the equity in the account falls below the maintenance requirement. The customer must then bring it up to the maintenance requirement—here 25%. Generally, when an account becomes undermargined, the margin clerk will issue what is known as a *margin call*. That is, he sends the customer a notice that the customer must deposit additional monies or his account will be liquidated.

Most brokerage firms have maintenance requirements that are greater than those of the New York Stock Exchange—usually, from 30% to 35% of the *current market value.* Thus, as a practical matter, a customer will get a *margin call* long before his account hits the NYSE maintenance requirement of 25%.

Restricted Accounts

An account may have no excess but not be on call. Such an account has a debit balance that is higher than the current loan value.

To Illustrate:

Current market value	$ 10,000
Less debit balance	6,000
Equity	$ 4,000

With a 50% loan value, the account is currently undermargined but not by enough to justify a maintenance call.

Should the customer decide to purchase additional stock, the brokerage firm requires margin only for the new purchase. It does not compel the customer to deposit sufficient funds to bring the entire account up to the margin requirement.

When a client *sells* a security from a restricted account, he is entitled to withdraw 50% of the proceeds. Any excess in this account is recomputed using the full proceeds of the sale. The customer may withdraw 50% of the proceeds of the sale or all the recomputed excess, whichever is higher.

Special Memorandum Accounts (SMAs)

In a restricted account, keeping track of the monies that the customer could have withdrawn is impossible. After a sale settles, the security position disappears, and the proceeds from the sale are merged with the account balance. To keep track of these entries, the *special memorandum account* (SMA) is employed. The SMA is *only* a bookkeeping account. Of and by itself, it does not figure into margin calculations. It is a way to record entries of monies the customer could have used. Either margin employees or computer programs keep track of the entries booked into and out of the SMA.

A CASE SUMMARY

A case example may tie together all we have said about margin accounts.

To Illustrate: With the margin rate at 60%, the loan value at 40%, client Compton purchases 1,000 shares of Seville Corp at $10 per share on margin.

Current market value: 1,000 shares Seville Corp at $10 $ 10,000
Equity: Compton deposits($10,000 x 0.60)   6,000
Debit balance: Firm lends ($10,000 x 0.40) $ 4,000

Compton will pay interest on the $4,000 borrowed.

Seville rises to $15 per share. Compton's account would show the following:

Current market value: 1,000 shares Seville Corp at $15 $15,000
Debit balance: Less borrowed amount   4,000
Equity $ 11,000

The loan value on $15,000 of market value is $6,000 ($15,000 x 0.40). Compton has borrowed $4,000 and therefore can borrow $2,000 more. This is the Regulation T excess. Compton can borrow the money or use it as a deposit on another transaction. If Compton decides to use the *excess* ($2,000) to purchase more stock, his *buying* power would be $3,333.33 ($2,000 divided by 0.6).

In other words, with the $2,000 Reg T excess, Compton can purchase $3,333.33 more security value. Assuming Compton does this, his account would have the following balances:

Current market value (CMV) $18,333.33
Equity   11,000.00
Debit balance $ 7,333.33

Account was		Borrow	New Purchase		Account is
$ 15,000 CMV			+ $3,333.33	=	$18,333.33 CMV
11,000 Eq	−	$2,000	+ 2,000.00	=	11,000.00 Eq
$ 4,000 Db	+	$2,000	+ $1,333.33	=	$ 7,333.33 Db

Proof: 40% of $18,333.33 = $7,333.33

At the present time the margin rate is 50%, and therefore the loan value is 50%. Using the current rates, Compton's account would have been as follows:

Current market value: 1,000 shares Seville Corp $ 10,000
Equity: Compton's deposit   5,000
Debit balance: Firm lends $ 5,000

Note that because the margin rate is 50% instead of 60%, the minimum Compton would have to deposit is $5,000.

Seville rises in value to $15 per share.

Current market value: 1,000 shares Seville Corp	$15,000
Equity	10,000
Debit	$ 5,000

The loan value (50%) on $15,000 is $7,500. Compton has borrowed $5,000 and therefore can borrow $2,500 more. If Compton uses the Reg T excess (the amount the debit balance is below the allowable loan value) to purchase more securities, the amount that can be purchased (buying power) without Compton's having to deposit additional funds is $5,000 ($2,500 divided by 0.5).

Not all transactions are profitable. Therefore, as the value of a security falls, the equity in the account also falls on a dollar-for-dollar basis. When the equity falls to a specific level, the client will be called to deposit additional money or equity.

To illustrate: Jim Nasium's account has the following values:

Current market value	$120,000
Equity	60,000
Debit balance	$ 60,000

If the market value of the account falls below $60,000, the account would have a negative equity or, to put it another way, the loan made by the firm to the client would be unprotected (known as *unsecured*). To protect against this event, maintenance rules are brought into play.

The maintenance rules used were written by the New York Stock Exchange. The exchange's maintenance rules state that the equity in the account must not drop below $\frac{1}{3}$ of debit balance or 25% of the market value.

As the market value falls, the equity falls. Therefore, to determine the level to which the market value can fall, you compute $\frac{1}{3}$ of the debit balance. This gives the minimum equity that the debit balance can support.

$$\frac{1}{3} \times \$60,000 \text{ Debit balance} = \$20,000$$

If the equity in this example falls below $20,000, the firm must call for more money. Let's assume the market value falls to $75,000.

Current market value	$75,000
Equity	15,000
Debit balance	$60,000

Since the equity cannot fall below $20,000, the firm must send a maintenance call. The amount of the call is determined by the minimum equity (25%) necessary to support the current market value.

$$\begin{array}{r} \$75,000 \\ \times \quad 0.25 \\ \hline \$18,750 \end{array}$$

Because $18,750 is the minimum equity required to support a $75,000 market value and because the equity is only $15,000, the firm will call for $3,750. After the funds are deposited by the client, the account has the following balances:

75,000	CMV			$75,000
15,000	Eq	+	3,750	$18,750
60,000	Db	−	3,750	$56,250
			(Amount deposited)	

Note that if the other test is applied ($\frac{1}{3}$ of debit balance), the balances in the account will satisfy it also.

$$\frac{1}{3} \times \$56,250 = \$18,750$$

The automated systems in the margin department make such calculations all day long. It would be easy for the margin staff to grow lax about the firm's accounts' compliance with regulations. The real job in margin is surveilling accounts and taking appropriate action when they are in trouble.

THE ROLES OF THE MARGIN DEPARTMENT

Account Maintenance

The margin department ensures that all the customer accounts are operating in accordance with the regulations. It reviews accounts, continuously computing excess and/or buying power.

Sales Support

Any one of a thousand questions may be directed to the margin department in a day. Reliable, accurate responses to these questions are vital to the overall operation of the firm. The account executive in particular turns to this department for information when soliciting orders from clients. For example, the account executive may be discussing a possible transaction with a client, such as buying 100 shares of XYZ and selling or writing a call on the stock. He must know what effect this transaction will have on the account.

Clearance for Issuance of Checks

In most retail brokerage firms, the branches must wire a message to the margin department for an *OKTP*. This message asks the margin employee to verify that an amount of money being paid to the customer is *"OK to pay."* Before the branch can draw the check, it must get the margin department's approval. In some firms, the amount is transmitted to the branch offices each morning, and the branches can pay the amount transmitted *without* approval.

Items Due

The nature of the securities industry results in the credit department staff spending a lot of time informing branch offices of *items due*. Items due are pending or actual deficiencies in customer accounts. Included in item-due messages are:

1. *Money due on T calls*—the sum a customer owes on a transaction.
2. *Money due on house calls*—the sum a customer owes to satisfy an equity deficiency (that is, the equity is below the minimum maintenance requirement).
3. *Stocks or bonds due to be delivered* by the client against a sale in the account.
4. Any other pending problem.

Someone at the branch, usually an account executive, must contact the clients and advise them of the discrepancies. The client's obligation is then to satisfy the discrepancy.

Extensions

Clients occasionally enter into a security transaction and, due to circumstances beyond their control, cannot satisfy the obligation in seven business days. In such a case, the firm, on instruction from the account executive and with the approval of the margin department, files a request for an *extension of time* with the appropriate self-regulatory organization—the NYSE, Amex, PCE, PHLX, NASD, and so on. If the request is granted, the client has additional time to satisfy the commitment. A customer is generally permitted to have five extensions per year on an industry-wide basis.

Close-Outs

If a transaction fails for any reason, the firm has to take the appropriate action and *close out* the transaction. If the client has failed to pay for a purchased security, the security is liquidated. In closing an unsatisfied purchase, the brokerage firm is said to *sell out* the purchased security. If the client has failed to deliver a sold security, the firm closes out the commitment. In closing out an unsatisfied sale, the firm is said to *buy in* (that is, the firm buys the security elsewhere and delivers to the buying firm).

Because the problem arises with the customer, the closing transactions must be effected in the customer's account. Any profit or losses from these close-out transactions that result from fluctuations in the security price belong to the customer. Naturally, customers are only too willing to take profits, but losses create problems for the brokerage firm. If the client does not honor the loss, the firm has to absorb it or go to court to collect.

Delivery of Securities

When a customer's securities remain in the firm's possession, the firm owes the securities to the customer and so has a custodian obligation. The margin department, therefore, also is responsible for the release of securities for delivery to clients. (Some customers request physical delivery of the securities at the time of purchase.) Securities can be delivered only if the client has paid for them in full.

A client who *sells* securities owes the firm delivery of the securities sold. Once delivery is made, the firm owes the customer the proceeds. A client who *purchases* securities on margin owes the value of the loan to the firm.

Certain securities, known as *registered securities,* must be sent by the brokerage firm (or by a depository on instructions from the brokerage firm) to a transfer agent. The transfer agent reregisters the security in the customer's name and mails the new security to the brokerage firm for delivery to the customer. Once these securities are delivered to the customer, the security is no longer reflected in the customer's account.

The margin department keeps track of all these entries, making sure that accounts reflect the correct balances. And "correct" is the key word. The margin department has the dual responsibility of protecting the firm's money *and* the customer's funds. The margin department must be aware at all times of *all* the rules affecting broker-customer relationships.

13   The Cashiers Department

After P&S has completed its function, within the industry-imposed time constraints, the reconciled transactions enter their settlement process. Each transaction being settled contributes to the movement of securities and monies. The orderly processing and control of the settlement date routine is the function of cashiers.

One of the major enemies of a brokerage firm, or any business for that matter, is *interest expense.* The minimizing of this, through the intelligent use of financial resources, is what the cashiers department does. This department is responsible for six functions:

- Receiving and delivering.
- Vaulting.
- Hypothecation of security for margin accounts (bank loans).
- Stock loans (borrowing and lending money and securities).
- Security (stock) transfer.

- Keeping track of reorganizations, tenders, and spin-offs.

These functions may be performed on the premises, through outside institutions, or through a depository. (Depositories are discussed later in this chapter.)

Of all the departments in the production cycle, the cashier function has been most affected by industry processing problems. Yet, as a group, the cashiers departments of the many firms have responded with viable new systems.

RECEIVE AND DELIVER

The efficient movement of securities and funds in and out of the firm is the key to a successful operation. The responsibility for the proper allocation of issues falls on the receive and deliver section.

The Settlement Cycle

After all transactions have been executed and compared, brokerage firms must eventually settle. Selling firms deliver securities to the buying firms, and buying firms pay the contracted amount to the selling firms when the delivery is effected. The settlement in some cases necessitates physical or actual delivery; in other cases, the delivery is made and paid for through book entry.

Physical delivery is conducted on a firm-to-firm basis. The receiving firm prepares checks on the morning of settlement day, payable to the delivery firm, and waits for the security to be delivered. Upon receipt of the security, the receiving firm releases the appropriate check. Because the amount of money for the transaction is determined from the firm's records, the importance of comparison discussed in Chapter 11 becomes apparent. If the delivery firm's records state a different sum to be received upon security delivery, the receiving firm will "DK" or "bounce" the delivery, thereby returning it to the selling firm without paying for it.

The clearing corporation made a major step forward when it offered netting and allotting and single security settlement. All transactions entering the clearing corporation's settlement cycle have been compared. Therefore, for each buyer there is a seller at an agreed price. The only difference that could exist between the many shares of a given issue that were traded is the execution price. Therefore, the clearing corporation establishes a common price for settlement purposes and then debits or credits the firm's account, the difference between their established settlement price, and one actual execution price. The clearing corporation can "net out" each firm's position in a particular security.

For example, trades settling for a given day in XYZ could be as shown in Table 13–1.

As a result of the netting and allotting process, two balance orders will be issued by the clearing corporation. One instructs Broker A to deliver 100 shares to Broker C @ $4,300; the other instructs Broker C to receive 100 shares from Broker A for $4,300. The clearing corporation debits and credits the firms accordingly (that is, credits A $150, debits B $200, and credits C $50).

Balance orders drastically reduced the number of deliveries that have to be made daily to settle transactions. Through this settlement process, called *netting,* firms are spared the need to receive and deliver securities that basically duplicate each effort. As a result of a firm's trading activity, the transactions in the same security are paired off, leaving a firm with one position per security to contend with. This position might be to receive, to deliver, or to be flat (buys equal sells).

Under the trade-for-trade and balance-order settlement, securities have to be delivered and paid for to satisfy the firm's obligations. If the firm is unable to deliver securities on settlement date, the procedure is referred to as a *fail.* The selling firm has a "fail-to-deliver," the buying firm records a "fail-to-receive."

Table 13–1. The Settlement Cycle

Transactions	Settlement Price	Adjustment
Firm A–B 100 @ $42\frac{1}{2}$	43	+ $ 50.00
S 300 @ 43	43	0
B 100 @ 42	43	+ $100.00
❑ Net seller 100 @ 43		+ $150.00
Firm B– B 300 @ 43	43	0
S 100 @ 43	43	0
S 200 @ 42	43	− $200.00
❑ Flat		− $200.00
Firm C–S 100 @ $42\frac{1}{2}$	43	− $ 50.00
B 100 @ 42	43	+ $ 100.00
B 100 @ 43	43	0
❑ Net buyer 100 @ 43		+ $ 50.00

When the selling firm delivers the security, the buying firm pays the money due, and both firms clean up these fails.

Functions of a Depository

Many of the instruments that the industry processes are represented by a legal document known as a certificate. The certificate represents physical evidence of ownership. Historically, the registration or possession, in the case of bearer instruments, has been required to prove the identity of the rightful owner.

As the volume of transactions in a given product increases, the ability to settle transactions through the delivering of securities becomes more and more cumbersome and error-prone. Concepts, like netted balance orders, proved to be only a stop-gap measure and was viable until the volume of transactions and the number of firms participating in the product prove netted balance orders to be inefficient. What becomes imperative is the immobilization of the certificate and the use of automation to record ownership. Enter the concept of a depository.

Depositories, such as Depository Trust Company, were formed to negate the need for brokerage firm to brokerage firm or firm and bank physical movement of securities. This is accomplished by the participating entities placing securities at the depository.

The depository registers the instruments in their nominee names and maintains the securities physically in their vault while carrying the depositing firm position on their book records.

With each participant's deposited security recorded on a master record, the depository's system will debit and credit these positions, according to the participant's instructions, to record security movement. These bookkeeping entries accomplish the same results that the physical movement of securities did formerly, but in an extremely efficient and less problem-prone environment.

To Illustrate: First Continental Bank and Trust sells 20,000 shares of E&B Satin Corp through the Giant Recker & Crane (GRC) brokerage firm. The trade was consummated between Giant Recker and Stone Forrest & Rivers, which is the buying firm representing its client, the Raechel Bank and Trust of North Carolina. If physical securities have to be delivered, the following steps would be followed:

1. First Continental Bank and Trust would deliver the shares to Giant Recker & Crane.

2. Giant Recker & Crane would receive the securities of E&B Satin Corp and deliver them off the account to Stone Forrest & Rivers.

3. Stone Forrest & Rivers would receive the physical certificates, making sure they were in proper negotiable form and send them to the transfer agent to be reregistered in the name of Raechel

Bank and Trust while, at the same time, receiving them into the bank's account.

4. Upon the securities being returned from transfer, Stone Forrest & Rivers would deliver the securities off the bank's account while sending the physical securities to the Raechel Bank.

Under the book entry system of the depository, each entity gives the depository instructions as to what is to occur.

To Illustrate: In one series of entries the *position* of First Continental is reduced by 20,000 shares and GRC is increased; GRC's position in E&B Satin Corp is then reduced and SFR's position is increased. SFR's position is then reduced and Raechel Bank and Trust's position is increased.

All of these debits and credits are entered in one evening *without a single physical share being touched.* The entries made on each participant's records are the same in both the physical and book entry methods, but without the need to handle securities. In one case delay the process due to the need to reregister the instrument.

From an operation's standpoint, the depository acts as an extension of the clearing firm's cashiers department. A firm may maintain securities on its premises, at a depository, at a commercial bank, or at any combination of these. The cashiers department is responsible for the control and movement of securities at each of these locations.

The depository acts as an extension of the firm's own cashiers department. On instruction from the firm's cashier, the depository submits positioned securities to a transfer agent for reregistration into the name of another. The firm can also instruct the depository to receive or deliver securities on its behalf. Movement from one booked position to another is increasingly a computerized activity.

Institutional Customers

Custodial and commercial banks are also participants in the depository process. They act on behalf of pension funds, insurance companies, and their own trust departments. These forms of accounts, known as *institutional accounts,* require the account manager to issue two sets of instructions for each transaction.

One set of instructions, for the brokerage firm, is an order to transact business. The other set, to the custodial bank, is to receive or deliver securities vs. payment. Depository Trust Company (DTC) and some other depositories offer a service that expedites the settlement of these transactions. DTC's service is known as the *Institutional Delivery Service* (ID).

On trade date plus 2 (T+2), the brokerage firm submits the details of the transaction to DTC which, in turn, transmits these data to the respective bank. If the bank agrees with the terms of the transaction, they do nothing. If, on the other hand, the bank does not agree, they "DK" or challenge the transaction. Challenged transactions are researched by the brokerage firms and corrections are made by either the firm or the bank.

Trades that are agreed to are settled by book entry. DTC debits and credits the respective bank and brokerage firm accounts for the securities involved in the transaction.

With the depository concept in place, the need to move physical securities is greatly reduced. Participating firms and, at some depositories, custodial banks, settle transactions via bookkeeping entry. The physical security never leaves the depository's vault. (See Figure 13–1.)

Clearing Corporation: Continuous Net Settlement

The *continuous net settlement (CNS)* system uses the facilities of a clearing corporation (clearing house) and a depository. As trades of a firm settling in a

Figure 13–1. ID Transaction Notification Process

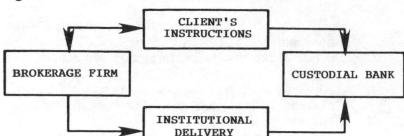

given security are netted to a single receive or deliver position, these positions are posted to the firm's account at the clearing corporation. Computer-produced tapes ("mag" tapes) are sent to the depository and passed against the firm's position account. If the net selling firm's position has the security available, it is used to clean up the settlement position. The clearing corporation then tells the depository the name of the receiving firm, and the depository enters the quantity received into that firm's account. This procedure permits the net seller and net buyer to settle their transactions without ever moving the physical security. If the deliverer does not have the security available, fails are opened on the clearing corporation record, a fail-to-deliver for the net seller and a fail-to-receive for the net buyer. The next day's settling trades are netted, but they also include the previous fail position. Therefore, the firm's account is always being updated.

   To Illustrate: On a given day, Firm A is a net receiver of 100 shares. The net seller is unable to deliver the security, so it becomes a fail-to-receive for Firm A. The trades from the following day reflect that Firm A will be a net deliverer of 100 shares. Under continuous net settlement, the previous day's fail-to-receive is included with the next day's settling trades. This results in Firm A being netted to a zero balance.

By including the previous day's fail position, if any, in with the next day's settling trades, the firm's position per security is constantly being updated, and the possibility of having multiple fails-to-receive and fails-to-deliver has been eliminated.

Money Settlement

With continuous net settlement, money settlement for transactions is against the clearing corporation. All transactions settled in all the CNS eligible securities are netted to one money settlement. The value of various securities received and delivered on behalf of a firm are netted into one "money receive" or "money payment" figure. If it is a "money receive," the clearing corporation pays the firm. If the value of the security received is greater than that delivered, the firm pays the clearing corporation. One money settlement suffices for all settled transactions.

The movements between the clearing corporation and the depository are controlled by the firm's cashiers department. It is the responsibility of the cashier to ensure that there are adequate securities on deposit at the depository and that only securities not needed for seg requirements (customer cash and margin accounts) are used to clean up transactions.

Good Delivery

A major duty of the receive and deliver section is to make certain that the securities flowing through the area are in good deliverable form.

Refer back to Figure 3–1, in Chapter 3. It is the face of a specimen stock certificate. Notice that it has a space for inserting the name of the owner (or owners) of the shares represented by the stock certificate. When the owner or owners sell the shares, they endorse the assignment form on the reverse side of the certificate. Figure 13–2 is a specimen assignment form. However, instead of endorsing the assignment form on the reverse side of the certificate, the owner may sign a separate assignment called a *stock power*. Figure 13–3 is a specimen stock power.

Figure 13–2. A Specimen Assignment Form

CONSOLIDATED EDISON COMPANY OF NEW YORK, INC.

A FULL STATEMENT OF THE DESIGNATION, RELATIVE RIGHTS, PREFERENCES AND LIMITATIONS OF THE SHARES OF EACH CLASS AUTHORIZED TO BE ISSUED AND THE DESIGNATION, RELATIVE RIGHTS, PREFERENCES AND LIMITATIONS OF THE SHARES OF EACH SERIES OF EACH CLASS SO FAR AS THE SAME HAVE BEEN FIXED BY THE BOARD OF TRUSTEES AND THE AUTHORITY OF THE BOARD OF TRUSTEES TO DESIGNATE AND FIX THE RELATIVE RIGHTS, PREFERENCES AND LIMITATIONS OF OTHER SERIES WILL BE FURNISHED TO ANY SHAREHOLDER UPON REQUEST AND WITHOUT CHARGE.

The following abbreviations, when used in the inscription on the face of this certificate, shall be construed as though they were written out in full according to applicable laws or regulations:

TEN COM	— as tenants in common	UNIF GIFT MIN ACT — ....Custodian................
TEN ENT	— as tenants by the entireties	(Cust) (Minor)
JT TEN	— as joint tenants with right of	under Uniform Gifts to Minors
	survivorship and not as tenants	Act................
	in common	(State)

Additional abbreviations may also be used though not in the above list.

For value received,_____ hereby sell, assign and transfer unto

PLEASE INSERT SOCIAL SECURITY OR OTHER
IDENTIFYING NUMBER OF ASSIGNEE

PLEASE PRINT OR TYPEWRITE NAME AND ADDRESS OF ASSIGNEE

*_____ Shares
of the Stock represented by the within Certificate, and do hereby
irrevocably constitute and appoint_____*

*Attorney to transfer the said stock on the books of the within-named
Company with full power of substitution in the premises.
Dated,_____*

NOTICE: THE SIGNATURE TO THIS ASSIGNMENT MUST CORRESPOND WITH THE NAME AS WRITTEN UPON THE FACE OF THE CERTIFICATE IN EVERY PARTICULAR, WITHOUT ALTERATION OR ENLARGEMENT OR ANY CHANGE WHATEVER.

THIS SPACE MUST NOT BE COVERED IN ANY WAY

Figure 13–3. A Specimen Stock Power

SAMPLE OF STOCK POWER

−Assignment Separate from Certificate.

For Value Received, ...

hereby sell, assign and transfer unto ....

....

....

....(...................) Shares of the ....

Capital Stock of the ....

standing in... name on the books of said...........................

.... represented by Certificate No. .... herewith

and do hereby irrevocably constitute and appoint ....

.... attorney to transfer the said stock on the books of the within named

.... with full power of substitution in the premises.

Dated ....

In presence of

....

When we say a certificate is a *good delivery,* we mean that the certificate is negotiable—that is, it is freely exchangeable. Stated another way, a certificate is a *good   delivery* if it contains the necessary endorsements and tax stamps on the reverse side of the certificate. If it does, then the certificate will be accepted by the buyer or his broker, or by the transfer agent for issuance of a new certificate in the new owner's name.

Many certificates are registered in the name of a securities house. These certificates are said to be in *street name.* They are a *good delivery* when they are properly endorsed by the firm and the necessary tax stamps are affixed.

However, stock certificates may also be registered in the names of persons other than brokerage firms—for example, in the names of individuals, partnerships, and corporations. Certificates may also be registered in the name of a *nominee*—that is, the name of a person or company other than the true owner. The purpose of registering the certificate in the name of a nominee is to speed up the handling of the certificate.

The Endorsements.   A certificate registered in the names of persons other than a securities house is a *good delivery* under the following conditions:

1 . The certificate has been signed by the owner.
2 . The owner's signature is guaranteed by a broker or a commercial bank. If the security is traded on the New York Stock Exchange, the signature guarantee must be by a member firm or by a commercial bank.
3 . The certificate has the necessary tax stamps affixed, or a notation that the tax has been paid, or a notation that the security is exempt from taxation.

Signature on the Certificate.   The   owner's signature must correspond to his name as it appears on the face of the certificate. For example:

1. A certificate registered in the name of *John Jones* must be signed *John Jones*—not J. Jones or Jack Jones.
2. A certificate registered in the name of *Dr. William Jones* should be signed the same way.
3. A certificate registered in the name of *Mrs. Mary Jones* should be signed Mrs. Mary Jones—not Mary Jones or Mrs. John Jones.

If a certificate is registered in the name of two or more persons as "tenants by the entireties" or as "tenants in common," the certificate must be signed by all the persons named thereon. A certificate registered in the name of a partnership, however, should be signed in the name of the partnership.

The receive and deliver section must be constantly on watch for securities that are not in good deliverable form—sometimes referred to as *dirty stock.* If either a customer or another firm attempts to deliver dirty stock, it is a *bad delivery.* In the case of a brokerage firm, the dirty stock has to be returned, or *bounced.* In the case of a customer, payment must be withheld.

The reason for either measure is that a bad delivery, if accepted, costs the firm money. Not only does the firm have to go to the expense of bringing the security up to good deliverable form, but it may not use that security until it is deliverable. If the firm pays the customer for the dirty stock, it actually loses the use of that money until the securities are deliverable. The firm might even have to borrow other securities for delivery elsewhere, thereby entailing the use of financing.

The Settlement Process

To assist the receive and deliver section, the personnel receive a computerized report each morning. The report contains lists of securities to be received and to be delivered. The delivery side prioritizes the needs so that securities coming into the firm can be utilized in the most efficient manner.

On the evening of Trade date plus 4, National Securities Clearing Corporation (NSCC) passes a settlement tape (a computer tape containing pending settling transactions) to Depository Trust Company (DTC). Items that can be "cleaned up" are settled; the remainder become part of settlement date processing (Trade date plus 5). These remaining transactions, plus transactions due for the next settlement date, appear on a listing known as the *projection report,* which is sent by NSCC to the clearing firms.

The receive and deliver section of the cashiers area receive this report the morning of settlement and use it in conjunction with their *receive and deliver (needs) report* to optimize security movement.

To Illustrate: The firm receives 100 shares of McKenna Inc. The analysis report shows that 100 shares are needed for trade settlement and 100 shares are needed for delivery to a customer. According to the projection report, McKenna stock has a delivery due on that day, but also shows a settling. A buy trade coming due the day after transactions in McKenna Inc is settled through CNS. What would you do?

If SFR delivers the stock out against the sell trade that is settling, the firm is not assured that they will receive the 100 shares from the next day's settling buy transactions. If the buy becomes a fail to receive, they cannot satisfy the customer's request for delivery.

If, on the other hand, the receive and deliver section uses the 100 shares of McKenna Inc to satisfy the customer, the settling sale trade will "fail" on settlement date. But, under continuous net settlement, it will be merged into the next day's settling buy, netting SFR out to a flat position.

VAULTING

At one time, security certificates were physically moved from one brokerage firm to another after a transaction. To facilitate such transfers, as well as to expedite other types of processing (such as dividend control), the firm kept both the customers' and the firm's securities on premises in a vault, called the "box." Securities belonging to customers were so recorded on the firm's records, so that the real owners, or *beneficial owners,* could always be identified.

The customers' certificates were, however, registered to the firm's name, that is, in *nominee name* (in name only). These securities could be delivered quickly by the firm. The beneficial owners were the customers. Yet, although the securities were registered, they were nonnegotiable and remained so until a transaction caused the beneficial owner to change.

When the security was sold, it was pulled from the vault and prepared for delivery. On settlement date, the certificates were delivered to the purchasing firm.

As trading volume increased over the years, physical delivery became cumbersome and, in some cases, almost impossible. Although physical delivery is still made in some cases, it is no longer the most common method.

Maintaining the "vault" (that is, keeping track of ownership) is one of the main functions of the cashier area. Securities must be very carefully tracked and recorded because they represent ownership, by either the firm or its customers.

Segregated (Seg) Securities

According to Regulation T, there are two classes of securities that must be locked up and cannot be commingled with the firm's own securities:

1. Customer's fully paid for securities.
2. Securities in a customer's margin account with a value that is more than 140% of the account's debit balance.

The firm must have these securities segregated from all others. They must be in an isolated location, and they may not be used for loan, short sales, or hypothecation. These securities are commonly nicknamed *seg,* short for "segregated."

HYPOTHECATION (BANK LOAN)

When customers purchase securities in a cash account and leave them in the possession of the brokerage firm, the securities may not be used to secure bank loans. The securities belong to the customer.

Firms that maintain inventory positions (dealers and market makers) finance their positions by pledging their own securities at a bank.

Firms whose clients acquire stock on margin pledge a portion of the customer's security to finance the customer's debit balance. As explained earlier, when customers purchase securities on margin, they pay for part of the purchase and the firm lends the rest of the purchase price to them. To lend money on a margin purchase, the firm pledges a portion of the customer's securities at a commercial bank and in doing so borrows the money.

The rules governing the amount of securities the firm can use are very strict. Securities that can be pledged in accordance with the rules is referred to as *free stock.* Stock that the firm cannot use is *segregated,* sometimes known as *seg securities.* If the firm pledges seg securities for a loan, it violates the seg requirements and is subject to fine, censure, or even suspension from the appropriate self-regulatory authority.

STOCK LOAN

Quite often a firm needs a particular security to complete a fail-to-deliver. (A fail-to-deliver occurs when a customer fails to deliver all the securities representing a sale he has made.) So the firm borrows the security from another firm, using cash as collateral. The firm lending the security obtains funds, which reduce its financing costs. Arbitrage firms (firms that specialize in temporary differences in the marketplace) frequently need securities to cover short positions; these firms borrow securities and return them when the arbitrage is completed.

To obtain securities, the borrowing firm sometimes enlists the services of a *finder,* who locates loanable securities for a fee.

Repurchase Agreements (Repos)

In a *repurchase agreement (repos),* a brokerage firm sells its inventory securities to a nonbank institution with the intention of repurchasing them at a later date. Government securities and commercial paper, for example, may be sold to organizations that have funds available for a short time. These institutions might be unable to invest their money otherwise, either because of prohibitive regulations or their unwillingness to be exposed to market risk. They often do, therefore, enter into repos.

The money is, in effect, lent for a day or two, and usually for no longer than a week. The brokerage firm and the lender agree on the terms and the interest rate at the time the trade is consummated. The firm's sell trade is processed as a same-day settlement, and the buy trade (or *buy-back*) is settled on the last day of the repo, as agreed upon. The difference between the two money amounts exchanged in the sell and buy transactions is the amount of interest charged on the money.

THE SECURITY (STOCK) TRANSFER

Among other things, the owner of stock has the right to receive dividends when they are declared. He also has the right to vote his shares of stock at stockholders' meetings.

So that the corporation will know to whom to pay dividends and to whom to send notices of meetings, as well as other notices and reports, the corporation keeps stock books. In these stock books, it lists the names of all persons to whom it has issued certificates of stock. You will recall that a certificate of stock is merely evidence that the person whose name is written on the face of the certificate is the owner of the shares.

The person whose name is listed in the corporation's stock books is called a *stockholder of record.* And, as we have learned, his name is on the certificate of stock issued by the corporation.

When the stockholder of record sells his stock, his rights pass to the new owner. However, the corporation cannot make the necessary changes on its stock books unless it is notified of the sale. The way the corporation is notified is when it receives a request to *transfer* the certificate from the former owner's name to that of the new owner.

As a practical matter, most corporations do not handle the mechanical details of transferring stock. Instead, the corporation arranges with a bank or trust company to act as its *transfer agent.* Thus, when you want to transfer stock, you send it to the corporation's transfer agent. (See Figure 13–4.)

Steps in the Transfer of Stock

1. The certificate of stock, together with transfer instructions, is sent to the corporation's transfer agent.
2. The transfer agent cancels the old certificate and issues a new certificate in the name of the new stockholder of record.
3. The transfer agent changes the corporation's stock book to show the name of the new stockholder of record.

In addition to having a bank as a transfer agent, most corporations also appoint another bank as *registrar.* The registrar's job is to keep an accurate record of the exact number of shares of stock issued by the corporation. This is done so that the corporation will not issue more shares than it is authorized to issue.

Before a new stock certificate can be delivered to the new owner, the ownership must be verified by the registrar.

Thus far we have spoken of stock being transferred into the name of the new owner (purchaser). However, the customer need not have the stock transferred into his name. Instead, he can have it transferred into his broker's name or into the name of a nominee.

If the customer has the stock transferred into his broker's name or his nominee's name, then the broker or nominee becomes the *stockholder of record,* and the customer, or actual owner, becomes the *beneficial owner.*

As *beneficial owner,* the customer retains his dividend, voting, and other rights. However, he has to act through the *stockholder of record* when he wants to exercise these rights.

Duties of the Transfer Section

It is the job of the stock transfer section of a securities house to send securities out for transfer and to get them back again. However, the clerks in this section cannot act on their own; they must have instructions. Usually, these instructions originate with the customer. For example, let us say that a customer has purchased 100 shares of XYZ common stock. The customer wants a stock certificate for these shares registered in his name. When the certificate is issued, he wants it delivered to him.

Here are the steps involved:

Step 1. The customer contacts his registered representative and gives him the transfer instructions. The registered representative, in turn, sends these instructions to the margin department, which must approve all transfer instructions.

Step 2. If the margin department approves the transfer instructions, it will then send them along to the cage (cashiers department).

Figure 13–4. Instructions to the Transfer Agent

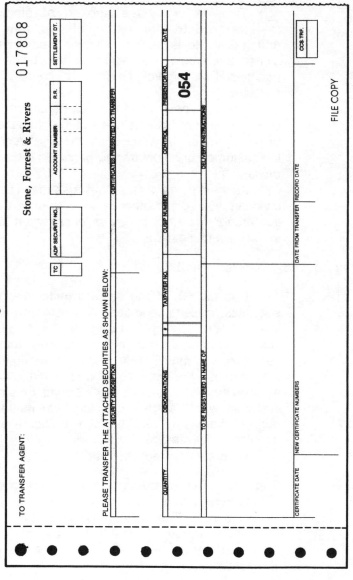

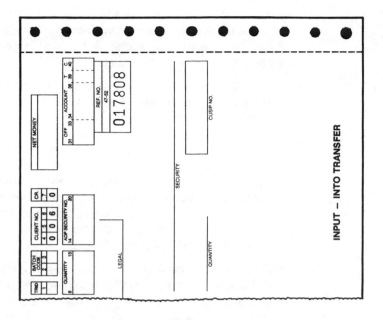

INPUT – INTO TRANSFER

Step 3. In the vault section of the cage, a clerk takes a stock certificate in *street name* from the active box and sends it along with the transfer instructions to the stock transfer section.

Step 4. When the certificate and the transfer instructions are received in the stock transfer section, a transfer clerk makes a record of the certificate number. He also examines the certificate to make certain that it is a *good delivery*. Then he sends the certificate and the instructions to the proper transfer agent. Most transfer agents, especially those of corporations whose stock is listed on the New York Stock Exchange, maintain offices within the vicinity of the Exchange. These offices are in New York City's financial district.

Step 5. When the new certificate comes back from the transfer agent, it goes again to the stock transfer section. There a clerk checks the certificate against his copy of the transfer instructions to make certain that the securities have been properly transferred. If there is any error in transfer—for example, the number of shares are wrong, or the owner's name is not properly stated on the certificate—it is the clerk's responsibility to catch the error. He then must return the certificate to the transfer agent and get back a corrected certificate.

Step 6. The transfer clerk sends the new certificate to the deliver section of the cage, which sends it out to the customer. You will recall that the customer in our example wanted the new certificate delivered to him. However, if the customer had wanted the broker to hold the certificate, then the transfer clerk would send it to the vault, where it would be stored.

Transfer Through the
Depository Trust Company

As you have read, the Depository Trust Company (DTC) makes transfers of stock for brokerage firms that have securities on deposit in their DTC accounts.

The stock transfer clerk, when he receives transfer instructions, fills in a transfer form. The clerk then attaches the transfer instructions to the form and sends it to the DTC, which then takes care of the transfer. When the DTC gets the new certificate back from the transfer agent, it sends it to the firm together with a copy of the transfer instructions.

REORGANIZATIONS,
TENDERS, AND SPIN-OFFS

Reorganizations are generally mergers in which the security of one company is surrendered for that of another. Company A merges with Company B to form Company C. Stockholders of Companies A and B may exchange their shares for stock in Company C.

To illustrate: Company A merges with Company B to form Company C. The *reorganizations section,* or *reorg,* is responsible for obtaining the necessary physical shares that represent the recorded ownership of the brokerage firm's customers and submitting them for the new shares. The new company's stock must be allocated among the stockholders of the merged companies in the proportion of their ownership. This task often involves computing full and fractional shares, because each customer *must* receive the amount deserved. Any error in the processing of the security could cost the brokerage firm money to correct.

Tender offers are similar to reorgs except that one firm makes an offer, usually in cash, for a certain number of shares of another company. Tender offers are usually made at prices higher than the current market price of the security. Stock owners may or may not want to accept the tender offer, and the company making the tender may accept all or part of the shares tendered.

In the event of a tender offer, the reorg section must, as part of its daily routine, do the following:

1. Secure enough securities to satisfy the instructions of the firm's customer.

2. Submit the securities to the tender agent within the allotted time.

3. Allocate the cash received among the participating customers.

4. Balance out, to a zero position, the shares submitted, the shares tendered, and the cash received per account.

All this usually has to be accomplished during heavy trading markets and changeable tender offers.

In a *spin-off,* a company separates, or "spins off," a subsidiary. The so-called *parent company* may spin off one or many subsidiaries in different share ratios. In so doing, it issues shares to its current security holders, and these securities must be credited to the appropriate customers' accounts.

14   The Stock Record Department

The stock record department keeps up-to-date records of each security the firm holds for its customers. The records are kept by name of the security. They show who owns the securities, how many shares, and where the securities are located (for example, in the vault or in stock transfer). In effect, then, the stock record department keeps an *inventory* of securities—where they are at all times.

Each business day, securities move into, out of, and through the firm. The security movements occurring during a day include, but are not limited to:

- Settlement of customer transactions.
- Settlement of firm transactions.
- Securities going into or out of transfer vs. the vault, depository, fail to receive, fail to deliver, customer receive, customer deliver, and so on.
- Securities going into or out of the vault vs. firm transfer, legal transfer, customer transfer, customer

receives or delivers, depositories, fail to receive, fail to deliver, and so on.

- Stock going out or being returned from stock loan, bank loan.

Each movement must be recorded and each movement requires two entries be made to account for it.

HOW THE STOCK RECORD IS KEPT

While the *margin department* keeps its records by name of customer, the *cage* keeps daily records. However, no attempt is made in the cage to keep these daily records either by name of customer or name of security. The records are kept by name of security only.

If you wanted to know which customers own, say, XYZ common stock and the number of shares each owns, you would have to go to the stock record department. There you could get the information easily and quickly.

The stock record department keeps its records by name of issuing company—for example, AB Company, GM Company, and WX Company. If the issuing company has more than one class of security outstanding, the stock record department keeps a separate record for each class—for example, AB common, AB $4 preferred, AB convertible preferred.

In addition to giving the names of the customers who own a particular security and the number of shares each customer owns, the stock record also shows where the security is located—that is, in the vault, in transfer, in fail to receive, and so on.

All securities movements are controlled by account numbers. These accounts fall into three categories:

- *Customer accounts* reflect positions of securities that the customer owns and that are maintained by the firm, or security positions that are owed to the firm by the client.

- *Proprietary accounts* are mainly the firm's trading accounts.
- *Street-side accounts* are "location" accounts, such as the firm's vault, transfer, and fail positions.

In most brokerage firms the stock record is maintained by computer. In some firms it may be kept on large ledger sheets or on cards. However, no matter in what form the stock record is maintained, the information is practically the same. For our purposes, we shall assume it is kept on large ledger sheets.

Figure 14–1 contains both long and short positions. The *long* position is also called the debit side; the *short* position is called the credit side. You will better understand the *long* position and the *short* position if you think of them in this way.

To illustrate: Customer WT539341 sends 1,000 shares of Caprice Corp to the firm to be deposited into the customer's account. The security is received into the firm's Dallas branch office's vault (DLV 1000).

Debit – A/C WT530341 1,000 shares
Credit – A/C DLV1000 1,000 shares

Long (Debit) Position

Think of *long* as meaning "we owe them." In other words, entries in the *long* position show the number of shares of a security the brokerage firm (we) owes its customers and other brokerage firms (them).

To illustrate: A customer, B. St. Clair, buys 75 shares of XYZ common, which he leaves with the brokerage firm. Until such time as the shares are delivered to St. Clair or he sells them, the brokerage firm (we) owes St. Clair (them) the 75 shares of XYZ common.

Figure 14–1. A Stock Record Ledger Sheet

XYZ COMMON					
LONG	8/5	8/6			
FAIL TO DEL.	...	100			
STOCKS BORROWED	100	200			
B. ST. CLAIR	75	125			
J. KEITH	100	/			
R. JOHNS	150	150			
S. BARTON	200	300			
TOTALS	625	875			
SHORT	8/5	8/6			
BOX	75	175			
TRANSFER	50	100			
SEGREGATION	200	200			
FAIL TO REC.	...	100			
STOCKS LOANED	100	/			
FIRST STATE BANK	100	100			
C. FRAZER	100	100			
E. SAWYER	...	100			
TOTALS	625	875			

Another customer, J. Keith, is the owner of XYZ common. He places an order with his brokerage firm to sell these shares, and the order is executed. Keith, however, is on vacation, so he does not send the stock to his brokerage firm. Because of this, the brokerage firm (we) cannot deliver the stock to the buyer's brokerage firm (them). This is a *fail-to-deliver*. Thus,

Keith's brokerage firm (we) owes the buyer's brokerage firm (them) 100 shares of XYZ common.

Short (Credit) Position

Think of *short* as meaning "they owe us." Thus, entries in the *short* position show the number of shares of a security others (they) owe the brokerage firm (us).

To Illustrate: S. Barton, who has bought another 100 shares of XYZ common, has given no transfer instructions to his brokerage firm. Until he does the stock will stay in the active box (vault). Although securities in the vault are actually in the brokerage firm's possession, the vault is treated as though it were separate and apart from the brokerage firm. Thus, the vault (they) owes the brokerage firm (us) 100 shares of XYZ common.

The customer, B. St. Clair, buys an additional 50 shares of XYZ common and gives instructions to transfer the shares to his name. The stock transfer section sends a certificate for 50 shares of XYZ common to the transfer agent. Along with it go instructions to issue a new certificate in B. St. Clair's name. Until the new certificate is issued, the transfer agent (they) owes the brokerage firm (us) 50 shares of XYZ common.

DAILY STOCK RECORD

Each day's movement is captured on the *daily stock record.* Each debit must be offset by a credit or credits, and vice versa. In this manner, all movements in a given security should balance: debits must balance with credits. The record is maintained in security order, then within security by account number, as shown in Figure 14–2. That figure represents accounts that had movements in Emily Frocks, Inc on May 11:

- 100 shares were received into account BS123412 and went to the New York vault NYV50000.
- Customer NY255412 bought 200 shares.
- Customers DC301521 and SV324451 sold a total of 300 shares for a net delivery of 100 shares.
- The net delivery for these transactions is satisfied by a delivery of 100 shares from the firm's position at Depository Trust Company DTC50000.
- Finally, 100 shares were delivered to account CG421312 from the Chicago vault CGV50000.

If one of these entries had not been processed, debits and credits would not equal each other. Any time an imbalance occurs, the stock record is said to be *out of balance.* To highlight this condition, computer program systems will "plug" in a special account known as a *break account.* Employees who work with this record know this account identifier on sight and immediately start to research the item.

For the firm to remain profitable, these "breaks" must be corrected on a timely basis. Open breaks become harder to trace as time goes by and could lead to other breaks, which only complicate the problem. As

Figure 14–2. Stone Forrest & Rivers' Daily Stock Record May 11, 198X for Emily Frocks, Inc.

Account	Activity	Previous Position	Debit	Credit	New Position
BS123412	Received		100		100 (Long)
NY255412	Bought		200		200 (Long)
DC301521	Sold	300 L		100	200 (Long)
SV324451	Sold			200	200 (Short)
CG421312	Delivered	100 L		100	----------
NYV50000		1,300 S		100	1,400
DTC50000		5,300 S	100		5,200
CGV50000		800 S	100		700

the problems compound, the record becomes less reliable, and this in turn jeopardizes the firm's ability to carry on business.

The stock record personnel are familiar with the account numbering methodology used by the firm. As they review the record each day, they are not only researching breaks but they are also looking for "illogicals," that is, entries that do not follow the firm's usual method of operations. While these are not breaks—debit equals credit—one of the debits or credits is incorrect. The staff still researches it and makes the correcting entries.

WEEKLY (MAIN) STOCK RECORD

In addition to the daily activity, the firm maintains a *weekly* or *main stock record.* It contains, in security order, the account number of every position for which the firm has a responsibility. This includes customer, street-side, and proprietary accounts.

SFR's weekly stock record for Emily Frocks (Figure 14–3) as of the close of business, May 11, 198X, reviews the stock's positions and their last activity date.

Figure 14–3. Weekly Stock Record for Emily Frocks

Date	Account	L	S	Date	Account	L	S
05-11-XX	BS123412	100		03-15-XX	PO613131	1000	
02-01-XX	HT164723	300		05-05-XX	SF703113	200	
05-11-XX	NY255412	200		01-03-XX	SF704113	1100	
02-15-XX	NY205543	1500		04-21-XX	LA804130	200	
05-11-XX	DC301521	200		05-11-XX	NYV50000		1400
05-11-XX	SV324451		200	05-11-XX	DTC50000		5200
05-11-XX	CG436313	1400		05-11-XX	CGV50000		700
04-05-XX	D2563112	200		05-05-XX	SFV50000		500
04-23-XX	H0512116	1800		04-21-XX	LAV50000		200

Note:

- The closing positions of the daily activity record appear as part of the weekly record.
- If the debit and credit columns were totaled, each column would total 8,200 shares.

At the close of business on the day the main record is produced, should any break accounts remain open, they would appear on the record. If the firm uses unique break account numbers, each identifying a different date, each break account would appear on the main record. The different break accounts greatly aid the stock record personnel in reconciling breaks that are open for more than one day.

THE AUDIT

The stock record department works in the shadow of one audit or another. Firms must audit their physical security positions quarterly. Once a year, an independent accounting firm performs a full audit, which includes all customer accounts, fail positions, and so on. In both kinds of audits, *all* the certificates are counted or verified in writing, and the results are compared to the stock record. Any discrepancy between the physical counts and the stock record position must be researched and explained.

Because the stock record is balanced daily, most errors are due to several commonplace circumstances:

- Both the original debit and credit entries were entered incorrectly.
- The wrong account was credited or debited the security.
- The wrong security was used to make delivery.

These types of errors are difficult to detect, because they do not create daily breaks. Even in these cases, however, an intelligent account numbering system will help. While scanning the record, an employee can spot improbable movements, check out possible errors, and take corrective action.

15   Cash Accounting

Besides balancing all securities movements, it is imperative that the firm balance all money movement also. This includes monies received from and paid to clients, other brokerage firms, banks, depositories, clearing corporations, and intrafirm account entries. As with security movements, each debit entry must have an equal and offsetting credit entry, and vice versa.

CREDITS AND DEBITS

Perhaps the most confusing fact to most people trying to grasp cash entries is how cash that belongs to them is a "debt." They see "their" money displayed as a credit because it is some other entity's view of it. For example, when you deposit money into your checking account, the bank "credits" your account. What the bank is actually doing is posting a liability to *their* records. In an account that the bank maintains for your benefit (your checking account), they *owe* you the amount of money deposited with them. "Your checking account" is, in reality, any account belonging to the bank and maintained by them for your use.

The next important concept that must be understood is that we value both cash and noncash items in dollars and cents. For example, $5,000 worth of stock means that the value of the security is $5,000. Stock is not cash even though it is valued in dollars.

To Illustrate: Customer Stasiak buys 100 shares of Tempo Music, Inc. at $50 per share. As the client is purchasing the stock, the account DL512644 is debited the stock and the money.

Stock			Money	
Debit	Credit	Explanation	Debit	Credit
100		Tempo Music, Inc.	$5,000	

As the account has a money debit balance, it means that Stasiak owes the firm money. When the client pays for the security, the account will be credited the money received.

Stock			Money	
Debit	Credit	Explanation	Debit	Credit
100		Tempo Music, Inc.	$5,000	
		Check 1-0113 Received		$5,000

With the check deposited, the Stasiak account has a "flat" money position and is "long" (debit) the stock. Stasiak wants the stock delivered as per the account's instructions. Since the account is in good order, Stone Forrest & Rivers delivers it.

Stock			Money	
Debit	Credit	Explanation	Debit	Credit
100		Tempo Music, Inc.	$5,000	
		Check 1-0113 Received		$5,000
	100	Tempo Music Delivered		

The account is now "flat" in both the security and money balances.

For each debit there must be an offsetting credit. When the purchase in the preceding account is posted, it is offset by crediting the firm's cash because it is paying the selling firm the money owed. The firm is now without their cash until the customer pays. When the client pays the money owed, the client's account is credited and the firm's cash account is debited.

Therefore, all money movements affect the firm's cash accounts. As these accounts represent assets, they are debited to increase their balance and credited when their balances are being reduced. As such, cash accounts must have a debit balance or be flat. Cash accounts with credit balances would mean that the firm has withdrawn more money than it had recorded as on deposit.

To illustrate: When a corporation pays a cash dividend, it pays it on a per-share basis to the registered holders. The corporation pays a dividend to Stone Forrest & Rivers for all the shares registered in their street name. The firm debits their cash account for the receipt of the money and credits a dividend payable account. Then, SFR credits the client's accounts the amount due and offsets these entries by debiting the dividend payable account. When and if any of the clients want the dividend paid to them, SFR will debit the client's account and credit the cash account the amount being paid.

DAILY ACTIVITY

Included in a day's work are the following cash entries:

Daily

- Trades settling in client's accounts.
- Trades settling vs. other firms.
- Clients depositing money into their accounts.
- Clients withdrawing money from their accounts.
- "Clean up" of fail-to-receives.
- "Clean up" of fail-to-delivers.
- "Set up" of the preceding two entries for new trades.

Weekly

- Payroll.

Monthly

- Charging interest expense to clients with margin debit balances.
- Crediting interest to clients that have cash in their accounts awaiting investments.
- Firm pays its usual bills, such as telephone, rent, electric, and so on.

Quarterly

- Credit clients for dividends paid by corporations.
- Charge clients for dividends owed to the firm.

Semiannually

- Interest paid by debt issuers to owners of the debt.

- Interest charged to clients for instruments not owned over record date.

Some of these entries, even though they are paid periodically, could occur at any time during the year. They could therefore occur on any day and be part of that day's work.

CLOSING THE BOOKS

In addition to the daily entries, the firm also performs monthly, semiannual, and annual routines. Those routines are known as *closing the books.*

Once a month the firm closes out its accounts to determine profit or loss. The revenue accounts include:

- Commission earned.
- Markup/markdown on principal transactions.
- Selling concessions.
- Interest earned on margin accounts.
- Interest and dividends earned on firm's proprietary positions.

The expense accounts include:

- Salaries.
- Heat, power, and light.
- Rent.
- Interest expense in carrying trade positions.
- Depreciation of equipment.

The profit and loss computations reveal whether the firm had a profitable or unprofitable month.

The net profit or loss is carried over to the firm's *balance sheet,* which is comprised of three areas: assets, liabilities, and net worth. The *assets* section includes:

- Cash.
- Accounts receivable (including clients' debit balance).
- Proprietary trading positions.
- Memberships (seats) on exchanges.
- Furniture and fixtures.
- Buildings or property owned.

The *liability* section includes:

- Accounts payable (including clients' credit balance).
- Loans from banks to cover the cost of positions.
- Mortgages.

The *net worth* section includes:

- Par value of stock (if brokerage firm is a corporation) or value of partnership.
- Contingencies for losses.
- Retained earnings.

The accepted formula for balance sheets is:

Assets = Liabilities + Net worth

Stone Forrest & Rivers prepares these reports on a monthly basis. Formalized statements (audited by an outside accounting firm) are developed on a semiannual and annual basis.

16 The Dividend Department

Stocks pay dividends out of earnings or retained earnings at the discretion of the corporation's board of directors. Bond interest is an expense to the issuing corporation. It must be paid or the bond holders can foreclose.

The function of the dividend/bond interest department is to insure that clients of the firm receive the proper dividend or interest payment when it is due. In addition, they must make certain that monies or securities owed to the firm on a dividend or interest payment are claimed and the claims satisfied.

The owner of stock in a corporation has several rights. One of these—and it is a very important one—is the right to receive dividends—whether cash or stock—when they are declared by the corporation.

As you have read, when a corporation declares a dividend, it pays the dividend to those persons whose names are registered on its stock books—that is, to the *stockholders of record*. If the purchaser of stock has the shares registered in his name, then he has no problem: The corporation sends him a check for his dividend.

However, many customers have their shares transferred into the brokerage firm's name. When stock is registered in a brokerage firm's name, that firm becomes the *stockholder of record*. The customer becomes the *beneficial owner.*

A corporation may issue two types of dividends for beneficial owners of its stock: cash and stock. In addition, it can also announce a stock split.

CASH DIVIDENDS

A company wanting to pay a cash dividend sets three critical dates: the declaration date, the record date, and the payable date.

To Illustrate: The McLaughlin Corp declares a $1.00 per share dividend on May 1 to holders of record on May 15. The dividend will be paid June 1. May 1 is the declaration date, the day on which the company announced the dividend. Registered owners, appearing on the registrar's books at the close of business May 15, will receive the dividend; this is the record date. Holders will be paid by the company's agent (known as the *dividend disbursing agent*) on June 1, the payment date.

The last regular-way trade date on which the security can be purchased and the new owner still be entitled to the dividend is May 8 (five *business* days before the record date of May 15). If the stock is purchased the next day, May 9, the settlement date of the trade would be May 16, the day after the record date. This first day on which a purchaser is not entitled to the dividend is known as the *ex-dividend date.*

The ex-dividend date is important not only because it marks the first day a purchaser is not entitled to the dividend, but also because the price of the stock in the marketplace is reduced by that amount, or to the next highest trading fraction before the opening of business that day.

To Illustrate: If McLaughlin Corp closed for trading on the evening before at a price of $90 per share, it would be adjusted by the marketplace in which it trades to $89 before the opening of business on the ex-dividend date.

This alteration, which is not caused by natural market forces, could trigger the execution of previously entered good-til-cancelled (GTC) buy limit and sell stop orders. To avoid these executions caused by an artificial stimulus, the limits on these types of orders are also reduced.

STOCK DIVIDENDS

Corporations, to conserve their cash, will sometimes pay shareholders a stock dividend. These shares are issued in percentages of shares outstanding.

To Illustrate: A 10% stock dividend means that, for each 100 shares you own, you receive 10 shares more.

What the corporation is actually doing is buying its own shares at the par value of the stock and paying for it out of earnings. It *does not* use cash, but makes bookkeeping entries. The marketplace accommodates this by viewing the dividend as follows: 100 shares at 90 is worth $9,000. Therefore, 100 shares (10% dividend) equals $9,000, each share being worth $81\frac{7}{8}$. The market price of the stock would be adjusted before the opening of business on the ex-dividend date, and pending GTC buy limit and sell stops adjusted accordingly.

STOCK SPLITS

When the price of a stock has risen significantly, the corporation may announce a stock split. What this accomplishes is to proportionately issue stocks in relation to the reduction of market value per share.

To Illustrate: In the preceding example, the stock was trading at $90 per share. If the company announced a three-for-one split, a stockholder of 100 shares worth $90 per share would receive 200 shares more. Then each of the 300 shares would be worth $30 (100 x 90 = $9,000, 300 x 30 = $9,000). Why split? Securities that trade at between $30 and $70 per share are more attractive to the public than stocks trading above $70.

The drastic drop in per-share market value on the ex-dividend date could have dramatic effects in margin accounts and bank loans, with borrowers having no method to cover the shortage until payable date. To avoid such problems, the ex-dividend date is moved to the payable date or the day after payable date. This way, when the ex-dividend reduction is applied, the borrower has the stock to satisfy the deficiencies.

For stock splits and stock dividends of more than 25%, the dividend process is as follows:

Declaration date May 1
Record date May 15
Payable date June 1
Ex-dividend date June 1 or June 2

Stock dividends under 25% follow the cash dividend process.

In the preceding example, someone purchasing the stock on May 8 would be entitled to the extra shares because they legally own the stock on the night of record, May 15. Someone purchasing the stock on May 9, with a settlement date of May 16, is actually purchasing the new stock, part of which is yet to be issued. This client is purchasing 100 shares of existing stock and a "rain check" on 200 shares more when it is issued. This "rain check" is known as a *due bill.*

A due bill is a promise to deliver additional shares when they become available. The purchaser's firm will not accept delivery of the stock from the seller's firm unless a due bill is included. On or shortly after the payable date, the purchaser's firm will surrender the due bill and receive the split stock, which is then booked to the clients' accounts.

THE ROLE OF THE DIVIDEND DEPARTMENT

The customer, as *beneficial owner,* is entitled to dividends. However, the brokerage firm will receive the dividends because it is the *stockholder of record.* When the brokerage firm receives a dividend check, it is the job of the dividend department to see that the check is in the correct amount and that the customer's account is properly credited.

To illustrate: A customer buys 100 shares of XYZ common and has it registered in the name of the brokerage firm. XYZ declares a dividend of 25 cents a share. It sends a dividend check for $25 (100 shares x 25¢) to the brokerage firm. There the check goes to the dividend department, which credits the dividend to the customer's account.

A brokerage firm may hold several hundreds— and even thousands—of shares of stock in the same corporation for the accounts of many customers. Normally, all these shares are registered in the brokerage firm's name (the *street name*). When the corporation declares a dividend on its common stock, it sends the brokerage firm *one* check for the dividends on all these shares.

Usually, even before the dividend check is received, a list is prepared. This list shows the names of the customers who own the stock, together with the number of shares each owns. When the check is received by the brokerage firm, the dividend clerk figures out how much should be credited to each customer.

To illustrate: A brokerage firm has 500 shares of XYZ common stock registered in its name. The shares are owned by four different customers.

> Customer A, 100 shares
> Customer B, 200 shares
> Customer C, 150 shares
> Customer D, 50 shares

XYZ declares a dividend of 25 cents a share and sends the brokerage firm a check for $125 (500 shares x 25¢). The dividend is then credited to each customer's account, as follows:

Customer A	100 shares	$ 25.00
Customer B	200 shares	50.00
Customer C	150 shares	37.50
Customer D	50 shares	12.50
Total		$125.00

Dividend Rate

The dividend rate is the amount of dividend the corporation has decided to pay. The dividend rate is given as a dollar and cents amount per share—for example, 20 cents a share or $1.25 a share.

By knowing the dividend rate, you can figure the amount of the dividend check your firm should get from the corporation.

To illustrate: A brokerage firm holds, as stockholder of record, 1,000 shares of XYZ common stock. XYZ declares a dividend at the rate of 25 cents a share. This means that the brokerage firm will receive from XYZ a dividend check for $250 (1,000 shares x 25¢).

So far, we have been studying how the dividend department credits dividends to the customers' accounts. Now, let us go on and study the other jobs the dividend department does. So that you will better understand these jobs, you will first have to learn some other things about the payment of dividends.

Declaration Date

When a corporation decides to declare a dividend on its common stock, it usually sends out a notice to announce the dividend. The notice is sent well in advance of the date on which the dividend will be paid. If a corporation declares a dividend payable on April 1, it may announce this on March 1. The date of the notice is known as the *declaration date.*

Copies of this notice are sent to the stock exchange on which the corporation's stock is listed, to the newspapers, and to financial publications. The stock exchange sends a summary of the notice to its members. The summary gives the brokerage firms this information.

Payable Date

When a corporation declares a dividend, it also fixes the date on which the dividend will be paid. This date is called the *payable date.*

The dividend department makes a record of this date. If it does not receive the dividend check on or shortly after that date, then it checks with the corporation to find out why the firm has not received payment.

Record Date

When a corporation announces that it will pay a dividend, the notice of dividend usually contains a sentence that reads like this: "The company will pay the dividend to all stockholders of record on the company's books on March 20."

Thus, we say that March 20 is the *record date.* This means that a stockholder's name must be registered on the corporation's stock books on or before March 20, if he is to receive the dividend.

In other words, the record date—here March 20—is a cut-off date. If a stockholder's name is not registered on the corporation's stock books by the record date, he will not receive the dividend.

To illustrate: XYZ Corporation announces that it will pay a dividend on April 1 to stockholders of record on March 20. You buy XYZ stock on March 13, but you do not have it transferred into your name until March 21. Since March 20 was the *record date,* you will *not* get the dividend from the corporation.

The dividend department has to keep track of the record dates set by corporations that are going to pay dividends. Then, if customers buy stock in these companies shortly before the record date, the dividend department will issue instructions to the stock transfer section to have the stock transferred by the *record date.*

Ex-Dividend Date

As you know, when your firm sells stock for a customer, it has five full business days to deliver the stock to the buyer. Actually, because Saturdays, Sundays, and legal holidays are not counted, at least a week usually elapses between the date stock is sold and the date it is delivered. Thus, as you can see, many times it will be impossible for the buyer to have the stock transferred into his name by the record date.

To illustrate: The record date is Friday, August 23. You buy the stock on Monday, August 19. The seller does *not* have to deliver the stock until Monday, August 26. Thus, it will be impossible for you to have the stock transferred into your name by August 23, the record date.

In view of this problem, the securities industry has established what it calls an *ex-dividend date.* This date is usually four business days before the record date. On that date, the stock is said to go ex-dividend. When a stock goes ex-dividend, it means that the stock is sold without the dividend.

Stated another way, a customer who buys stock between the ex-dividend date and the record date is not entitled to receive the dividend. However, during this four-day period, when the stock is selling ex-dividend, the price of the stock is reduced by the dividend rate.

To Illustrate: Friday, August 23, is the *record date,* and the *dividend rate* is 50 cents a share. On Monday, August 19, the stock will sell *ex-dividend.* If the price of the stock on that day is $50 a share, it will be reduced to $49.50 a share.

DEPOSITORIES

All stock maintained with a depository, such as the DTC, is transferred into the name of its nominee. When a corporation declares a dividend, the DTC receives a single check for the dividends on this stock. It then credits each brokerage firm with the amount to which it is entitled. The firm's dividend department, in turn, credits the dividends to each customer's account.

CLAIMING DIVIDENDS FOR CUSTOMERS

Most claims for dividends arise because the stock was not transferred by the record date. For example, if a customer buys stock a day or two before the *ex-dividend* date, it may not be possible to get the stock transferred before the record date.

The customer bought his stock before it went ex-dividend, so he's entitled to the dividend. However, the corporation's books did not show him as the *stockholder of record* on the record date. Thus, the corporation will pay the dividend to the person who was the stockholder of record on that date.

When this happens, it is the job of the dividend department to claim the dividend from the previous

Figure 16–1. A Dividend Claim Form

BROKER & CO.

MEMBERS NEW YORK STOCK EXCHANGE

When the books of the Company closed for the current dividend on the shares of stock indicated below, the certificates for the shares, registered in your name, were not transferred to the purchaser's name on or before the date of record in order for the purchaser to receive the dividend directly from the Company.

No. Shares	Description of Stock	Ctf. No. Registered in your name	Div'd Rate	Record Date	Payable Date

Although you sold the shares before the date of record, you were the registered owner on the books of the Company and therefore received, or will receive, a dividend from the Company on the aforementioned shares to which you are not entitled.

To settle the claim made on us by the actual owner of the shares on the date of record, may we ask that you send us this dividend after you have received it from the Company. By so doing we guarantee to hold you free and harmless from any further claim in the matter.

Very truly yours,

Figure 16–2. A Dividend Claim Form

BROKER & CO.

MEMBERS NEW YORK STOCK EXCHANGE

Dear Sirs:

On_____ when record of
stockholders was taken by_____for
a dividend of_____per share on their
_____ stock , payable_____, we or a client
of ours held_____shares, which was registered in the
name of_____
_____

　　　　　　We wish to claim the above dividend amounting to
$_____and would appreciate your check therefor, in consideration
of which we agree to hold you free from all claims for loss or damage
that may arise by reason of your complying with our request.

Very truly yours,

_____
Firm Signature

Certificates presented:
Letter of Evidence Presented:
Certificate numbers:

stockholder of record. If such stockholder is an individual, the dividend clerk makes the claim against this individual. On the other hand, if the previous stockholder of record is a brokerage firm, the dividend department claims the dividend from that firm. Figures 16–1 and 16–2 are specimen forms used to claim dividends.

BOND INTEREST

Government, municipal, and corporate bonds are usually structured to pay interest every six months. The payment periods are included in the bond's description; for example, "JJ" means January-July, "MS" means March-September, and so on. The actual or true record date is the night before payable. Therefore, whoever has his name registered on the security will receive the interest payment.

Note: Some bond transfer agents close their books—that is to say, will not accept bonds for transfer—one week before record date. This gives them time to process the then pending transfers.

17   The Proxy Department

The main function of the proxy department is to act as an intermediary between corporations and their stockholders with respect to voting rights, corporate reports, and so forth. Because many stockholders have their shares registered in the names of brokerage firms, corporations are unable to communicate directly with these stockholders. Instead, a corporation has to send the notices, reports, and other material to the brokerage firms (stockholders of record) whose names appear on the corporation's list of stockholders. The proxy departments of these firms send these materials to the firm's customers who are the actual owners (beneficial owners) of the stock. And when these customers want to give instructions on how their shares are to be voted at the meeting, they send back their instructions to the proxy department, which forwards them to the corporation.

Many stockholders keep their shares in the name of a brokerage firm. When stock is registered in the name of a brokerage firm (the street name), the firm becomes the *stockholder of record* and the customer becomes the *beneficial owner*. The stockholder as the beneficial owner does *not* lose his voting rights, but the situation does create problems of communication between the corporation and its stockholders. This is where the proxy department steps in to help the corporation and the stockholders.

STOCKHOLDER VOTE BY PROXY

Most corporations normally hold stockholders' meetings each year. At the meeting, the stockholders are asked to vote for the election of directors. They may also be asked to vote on other matters for which their approval is required by law.

A stockholder may, if he so wishes, attend the meeting in person and there cast his vote. Actually, however, very few stockholders personally attend meetings of stockholders. Instead, most stockholders vote by *proxy;* that is, the stockholder appoints another person to vote for him.

THE PROXY

The word *proxy* has two meanings. Generally, it means a person who is authorized to act for another. Thus, a person who is authorized to vote at a meeting of stockholders for an absent stockholder is called a *proxy*.

To illustrate: You are a stockholder of XYZ Corporation, and you have been informed that the corporation will hold a meeting of stockholders on a certain date. However, you are unable to attend the meeting in person. So you appoint John Doe to vote your stock at the meeting. John Doe is your *proxy*.

On the other hand, the written authorization that a stockholder gives to another person is also called a *proxy*. When signed by the stockholder, this authorization (proxy) permits the person named therein to vote in the place of the absent stockholder at the meeting of stockholders. Figure 17–1 is a specimen proxy.

Study Figure 17–1. Notice that it has spaces for the stockholder to indicate how he wants his shares voted on the matters that will come before the meeting. Notice, too, that it authorizes certain named persons to vote for the absent stockholder at the meeting. In other words, the proxy serves as both a ballot and an authorization.

When a corporation decides to hold a meeting of stockholders, it is required by law to send a notice of

Figure 17–1. A Specimen Proxy

MANAGEMENT PROXY—THE ABLE & BAKER CORPORATION
PROXY FOR ANNUAL MEETING OF STOCKHOLDERS
TO BE HELD APRIL 27, 19..

The undersigned hereby constitutes and appoints JON VAN KECK, N. HIRAM-SHORE and THOMAS WHITE, and each of them, with power of substitution, as attorneys and proxies to appear and vote all of the shares of stock standing in the name of the undersigned, at the Annual Meeting of Stockholders of The Able & Baker Corporation, to be held at 999 The Street, Your City, Your State, on Wednesday, April 27, 19.., at 10:00 A.M., and at any adjournments thereof:

1. FOR ☐ AGAINST ☐ adoption of a By-law amendment that would decrease from nine to eight the number of Directors. (Management favors a vote "FOR".)

2. WITH ☐ WITHOUT ☐ authority to vote for the election of directors. (Management favors "WITH.")

3. FOR ☐ AGAINST ☐ approval of the appointment of A.J. & Co., as auditors for the Corporation.

4. Upon such other business as may properly come before the meeting or any adjournment thereof.

The shares represented by this proxy will be voted as specified. If no choice is specified, the proxy will be voted FOR Items (1) and (3) and will be deemed to appoint the proxies WITH authority to vote for the election of directors.

The undersigned hereby acknowledges receipt of the Notice of Meeting and Proxy Statement.

Dated ...., 19...

....

(Please sign name exactly as it appears hereon.)

Figure 17–2. A Specimen Notice of a Stockholders' Meeting

THE ABLE & BAKER CORPORATION
NOTICE OF ANNUAL MEETING OF STOCKHOLDERS

NOTICE IS HEREBY GIVEN that the Annual Meeting of Stockholders of THE ABLE & BAKER CORPORATION will be held at the principal office of the Corporation, 999 The Street, Your City, Your State, on Wednesday, April 27, 19...., at 10:00 A.M., for the following purposes:

1. To consider and act upon the adoption of a proposed By-law amendment that would decrease from nine to eight the number of Directors.

2. To elect eight Directors of the Corporation.

3. To consider and act upon the approval of A.J. & Co., as auditors for the Corporation.

4. To transact such other business as may properly come before the meeting, or any adjournment or adjournments thereof.

Only stockholders of record at the close of business on March 18, 19.... will be entitled to vote at the meeting.

If you do not expect to be present in person at the meeting, please sign, date and fill in the enclosed proxy and return it by mail in the enclosed addressed envelope.

By Order of the Board of Directors

Robert Pratt, *Secretary*

Your City, Your State

March 25, 19....

---

the meeting to each stockholder. Figure 17–2 is a specimen notice of meeting. Notice that it tells the stockholder the place, time, and date of the meeting. In addition, it tells him what matters will come before the meeting for a vote.

THE RECORD DATE

The *record date* is a date fixed by the corporation for determining which stockholders shall be eligible to vote at the meeting of stockholders.

Normally, a corporation will fix a date from 10 to 40 days before the date of the meeting as the record date. This means that a stockholder's name must be listed on the corporation's stock books on that date if he is to be entitled to vote at the meeting. Stated another way, the record date acts as a cutoff date. If a stockholder's name is not listed on the corporation's stock books by that date, he usually will not be allowed to vote at the meeting.

To illustrate: XYZ Corporation announces that it will hold a meeting of stockholders on April 1. It fixes March 20 as the date for determining which stockholders may vote at the meeting. You buy XYZ stock on March 13, but it is not transferred into your name until March 21. Because March 20 is the *record date,* you cannot vote your shares at the meeting on April 1. However, you may ask the seller to give you a proxy and in that way you can vote at the meeting.

HOW THE PROXY DEPARTMENT HELPS CORPORATIONS

As you have read, a corporation recognizes only those stockholders whose names are listed on its stock books. These are the so-called *stockholders of record.* Thus, if you own stock in a corporation and the stock is registered in your name, there is no problem: The corporation will send directly to you the notice of meeting, the proxy, and all other proxy materials.

However, if you have your stock listed in the name of a brokerage firm, then that firm is the *stockholder of record*—and you are the *beneficial owner.* In that case, the corporation will send the notice of meeting and other materials to the brokerage firm.

Many corporations are aware of this practice of customers keeping their stock in the names of brokerage firms. So that these customers—the *beneficial owners*—will get the notices of meeting and other materials, most corporations get in touch with the brokerage firms and ask for their cooperation. Here is what they do:

Several days before the record date, a corporation will inform the proxy departments of brokerage firms that the corporation is going to hold a meeting of stockholders. At the same time, it will ask the proxy departments to let it, the corporation, know how many sets of notices of meetings, proxies, and other material the proxy departments will need for their customers—the *beneficial owners* of the corporation's stock.

When a proxy department receives this notice, it will have prepared a list of customers who own the corporation's stock, together with the number of shares each customer owns. From this list, the proxy department knows how many sets of material it will need for its customers. It orders these sets of material from the corporation.

As quickly as it can, the corporation sends the sets of material to the proxy department which, in turn, mails each customer a set of material.

Each customer who wants to vote at the stockholders' meeting by proxy checks the proper places on the proxy, signs it, and sends it back to the proxy department. When the proxy department receives the customer's instructions, it then sends a proxy to the corporation. In that way, the customer is able to exercise his voting right without actually being present at the meeting of stockholders.

Because the brokerage firm's name appears on the corporation's stock books as the *stockholder of record,* it must sign the proxy. Thus, when a customer sends back his signed proxy, the proxy department fills in a blank proxy in accordance with the customer's instructions and has it signed in the name of the brokerage firm. It is this proxy, signed in the name of the brokerage firm, that the proxy department sends to the corporation.

If a customer does not give his brokerage firm instructions on how to vote, the brokerage firm may usually vote the customer's shares for him. However, a brokerage firm may not do this if the matters to be voted on at the stockholders' meeting affect the legal rights of the stockholders—for example, a merger of the corporation with another corporation.

Glossary

Accrued Interest. The amount of interest that the buyer owes the seller on transactions involving fixed income securities, such as most bonds and notes.

Add by Seller. Form submitted by the selling firm (two days after trade date) to compare trades *not* previously submitted to National Securities Clearing Corporation (NSCC).

Added Trade Contract. The last in a series of contract reports rendered by NSCC. It contains the totals of previously compared trades from the regular way contract, supplemental contract sheets, and the trades compared through QT, DK, and CHC processing.

ADR. *See* American Depository Receipt.

Advisory Processing. Procedure by which the opposing firm's version of a trade is accepted by the named firm. Advisory notices accompany regular way contract reports received from NSCC.

Agency Transaction. A trade in which the firm operates as a broker, that is, it executes trades as an agent and charges a commission for the service.

All or None. A phrase used in certain underwritings and on some orders. In an underwriting, it is an instruction by corporation to a stand-by underwriter to take *all* of the forthcoming issue *or none*. On large-quantity orders, it is an instruction to fill *all* of the order *or none* of it.

American Depository Receipt (ADR). A share of stock that is issued by an American bank and that is backed by foreign securities on deposit.

American Stock Exchange (Amex). Located at 86 Trinity Place, New York, New York, a major stock and option exchange.

Asked. The offer side of a quote or the selling price. A quote represents the highest bid and lowest asked (offer) available in the marketplace at a given point in time.

As-of. A term used to describe any trade processed not on the actual trade date, but "as of" the actual trade date.

Balance Sheet. An accounting statement reflecting the firm's financial condition in terms of assets, liabilities, and net worth (ownership). In a balance sheet, Assets = Liabilities + Net Worth.

BAN. *See* Bond Anticipation Note.

Banker Acceptance. A discounted debt instrument used in international trade to expedite payment of goods in transit between exporting and importing countries.

Basis Price. A method of pricing municipal bonds, T bills, and certain other instruments. It is an expression of yield to maturity.

Bearer Form. Unrecorded security ownership. The individual "bearing" the instrument is assumed to be the owner.

Bearer Instrument. Any instrument (security) in bearer form.

Beneficial Owner. The owner of a security who is entitled to all the benefits associated with ownership. Customers' securities are often registered not in the name of the customer, but rather in the name of the brokerage firm or the central depository. Even so, the customer remains the real or beneficial owner.

Bid. The buy side of a quote. A quote is comprised of the highest *bid* (price at which someone is willing to buy) and lowest asked (price at which someone is wiling to sell).

Big Board. A popular name for the New York Stock Exchange.

Blotter. Another name for a listing used in operations. A "blotter" usually carries trades and customer account numbers, segregated by point of execution.

Blotter Code. A system by which trades are identified by type and place of execution. The code enables firms to "balance" customer-street-side trades.

Blue Sky Rules. Security rules of the various states. If a new issue is being sold interstate and has a value of more than $1,500,000, it must be approved for sale in each state. This process is known as "blue skying."

Bond. A debt instrument; a security that represents the debt of a corporation, a municipality, the Federal government, or any other entity. A bond is usually long-term in nature—10 to 30 years.

Bond Anticipation Note (BAN). A short-term municipal debt instrument.

Book-Value. A value computed by subtracting the total liabilities from the value of all assets on the balance sheet, then dividing by the number of common shares. This is an accounting term that has no relation to the securities market value.

Boston Stock Exchange (BSE). An equities exchange in Boston, Massachusetts.

Box. Another name for vault; where securities are maintained for the firm.

Breakpoint. A purchase of shares in an open-end investment company mutual fund that is large enough to entitle the buyer to a lower sales charge. A series of breakpoints is established by the fund, at each of which the charge is reduced.

Broker. (1) An individual who buys or sells securities for customers (a stockbroker). (2) On an exchange one who executes public orders on an agency basis (a floor broker or commission house broker). (3) As a slang term, a firm that executes orders for others (a brokerage firm).

Broker's Call Rate. The rate that banks charge brokerage firms for the financing of margin accounts and inventory positions.

Brokerage Firm. A partnership or corporation that is in business to provide security services for a general marketplace.

BSE. *See* Boston Stock Exchange.

Buying Power. In a margin account, the maximum dollar amount of securities that the client can purchase or sell short without having to deposit additional funds.

Call (Option). An option that permits the owner to buy a contracted amount of underlying security at a set price (strike or exercise price) for a predetermined period of time (up to the expiration date).

Callable. A securities feature that allows the issuer to retire the issue when desired. Should the issue be called, the issuer usually pays a premium.

Capital Gain. A trading profit. Trading gains that occur in six months or less are short-term capital gains; those that occur in periods longer than six months are long-term capital gains. Short-term and long-term capital gains are treated differently for tax purposes.

Capital Loss. A trading loss. Losses are long- or short-term as are gains. *See* Capital Gain.

Capital Stock. The common and preferred stock of a company.

Capitalization. The total dollar value of all common stock, preferred stock, and bonds issued by a corporation.

Cash Account. A customer account in which all securities purchased must be paid for in full by the fifth business day but no later than the seventh business day after trade.

Cash Dividend. Dividends that corporations pay, on a per-share basis, to stockholders from their earnings.

Cash Sale. A trade that settles on trade date and that is used in equities at the end of the year for tax purposes.

CBOE. *See* Chicago Board Option Exchange.

CBT. *See* Chicago Board of Trade.

Certificate. The physical document evidencing ownership (a share of stock) or debt (a bond).

Certificate of Deposit (CD). A short-term debt instrument issued by banks. CDs of larger denominations are negotiable and can be traded in the secondary market.

CFTC. *See* Commodities Future Trading Commission.

Chicago Board of Trade (CBT). A major commodity exchange located at 141 East Jackson Boulevard, Chicago, Illinois.

Chicago Board Option Exchange (CBOE). Listed option trading was originated by this marketplace on April 26, 1973.

Chicago Mercantile Exchange. A major commodity exchange in Chicago, Illinois.

Clearing Corporations. A central receive and distribution center operated for its members, who are made up of various brokerage firms. Many offer automated systems that expedite comparison procedures. Among these are NSCC (National Securities Clearing Corporation) and OCC (Options Clearing Corporation).

Clearing House Comparison (CHC). A form used to submit trades to NSCC that have missed the normal entry methods. Such trades enter the system on the third business day of the trade cycle.

CME. *See* Chicago Mercantile Exchange.

CNS. *See* Continuous Net Settlement.

Collateral. An asset pledged to support a loan.

Collateral Trust Bond. A debt instrument issued by one corporation and backed by the securities of another corporation.

COMEX. A commodity exchange located at 4 World Trade Center, New York, New York.

Commercial Paper. A short-term debt instrument issued by corporations. Its rate of interest is set at issuance and can be realized only if held to maturity.

Commission. (1) The amount charged by a firm on an agency transaction. (2) The method by which account executives are compensated.

Commission House Broker. A floor broker who is employed by a brokerage house to execute orders on the exchange floor for the firm and its customers.

Commodities Future Trading Commission (CFTC). Responsible for the enforcement of rules and regulations of the futures industry.

Common Stock. A security, issued in shares, that represents ownership of a corporation. Common stockholders may vote for the management and receive dividends after all other obligations of the corporation are satisfied.

Comparison. The process by which two contra brokerage firms in a trade agree to the terms of the transaction. Comparison can be either through a clearing corporation or on a trade-for-trade basis (that is, ex the clearing corporation).

Confirmation. A trade invoice, issued to customers of brokerage firms, that serves as written notice of the trade, giving price, security description, settlement money, trade and settlement dates, plus other pertinent information.

Continuous Net Settlement (CNS). The process by which a previous day's fail positions are included in the next day's settling positions.

Convertible Issue (Bond). A security's feature that permits the issue holder to convert into another issue, usually common stock. This privilege can be used only once. The preferred stock- or bondholder can convert from that issue to another, but not back.

Cooling-Off Period. The period, usually 20 days, between the filing of the registration statement on a new issue with the SEC and the effective date of the offering.

Corporate Bond. A debt instrument issued by a corporation. It is usually fixed income, that is, it carries a fixed rate of interest. From issuance, the life of a bond may be as long as 30 years.

Credit Balance. The funds available to a client in a cash or margin account. In a short sale, this balance represents the customer's liability.

Cumulative Preferred. A preferred stock feature that entitles the holder to the later payment of dividends that were not paid when due. The dividends are, in this sense, "cumulative." The dividends accumulate and must be paid (along with present dividends) before common stockholders may receive any dividends.

Curb Exchange. An archaic name for the American Stock Exchange (Amex).

CUSIP. The Committee on Uniform Security Identification Procedure, an interindustry security coding service. Each type of security has its own unique CUSIP number.

Day Order. An order that, if not executed on the day it is entered, expires at the close of that day's trading.

Day Trade. The buying and selling of the same security on the same day.

Dealer. A firm that functions as a market maker and that, as such, positions the security to buy and sell versus the public and/or brokerage community.

Debenture Bond. A debt that is issued by a corporation and that is backed or secured by nothing but the good name of the issuing company.

Debit Balance. The amount of loan in a margin account.

Deed of Trust. *See* Indenture.

Delete of Compared. A form, as well as a process, used to delete trades that were compared by mistake through NSCC.

Depository. A central location for keeping securities on deposit.

Depository Trust Company (DTC). A corporation, owned by banks and brokerage firms, that holds securities, arranges for their receipt and delivery, and arranges for the payments in settlement.

Designated Order Turnaround (DOT). An order routing and execution reporting system of the NYSE. Orders up to 599 shares may be entered by member firms through this system.

Director. A corporate board member elected by the stockholders.

Dividend. A portion of a corporation's assets paid to stockholders on a per-share basis. Preferred stock is supposed to pay a regular and prescribed dividend amount. Common stock pays varying amounts when declared.

DK. *See* Don't Know.

DNI. *See* Do Not Increase.

DNR. *See* Do Not Reduce.

Do Not Increase (DNI). An instruction that informs order handling personnel not to increase the quantity of shares specified on the order in the event of a stock dividend. DNI is placed on buy limit, sell stop, and stop limit GTC orders.

Do Not Reduce (DNR). An instruction that informs the order handling personnel not to reduce the price of the order by the amount of dividends, if and when paid by the corporation. DNR is placed on buy limit, sell stop, and sell stop limit GTC orders.

Don't Know (DK). A term used throughout the industry meaning "unknown item." On the Amex, the term applies to equity transactions that cannot be compared by the morning of trade date plus three business days. It is also used over the counter for comparison purposes.

DOT. *See* Designated Order Turnaround.

DTC. *See* Depository Trust Company.

Due Bill. An IOU used primarily in the settlement of trades involved in dividend and split situations, when the security is unavailable for delivery.

Effective Date. The first date after the cooling-off period of a new issue that the security can be offered.

Equipment Trust Bonds. Debt instruments that are issued by some corporations and that are backed by "rolling stock" (such as airplanes or locomotives and freight cars).

Equity. The portion in an account that reflects the customer's ownership interest.

Escrow Receipt. A guarantee of delivery issued by a qualified bank to a clearing corporation, such as OCC, on behalf of the bank's customer. The member brokerage firm acts as a conduit for this document.

Ex-Dividend Date. The first day on which the purchaser of the security is not entitled to the dividend. It is also the day that price of the security drops to the next highest fraction of the dividend amount.

Exercise Price. *See* Strike Price.

Expiration Month. The month in which an option or futures contract ceases to exist (expires).

Face Value. The debt (or loan) amount that appears on the face of the certificate and that the issuer must pay at maturity.

Factor Table. A table used to compute the outstanding principal on Pass-Throughs—Ginnie Maes, Freddie Macs, and Fannie Maes.

Fail. A transaction that is not settled on the appropriate day.

Fail-to-Deliver. An unfulfilled commitment by a selling firm to deliver a security if the parties to the trade are unable to settle on the settlement date.

Fail-to-Receive. An unfulfilled commitment by a purchasing firm to receive a security that is not settled on the settlement date.

Fast Automatic Stock Transfer (FAST). A service offered by DTC.

Fed Funds. Same-day money transfers between member banks of the Federal Reserve System by means of the Fed wire. These transfers are draw downs and loans of reserve deposits.

Figuration. The computation of trades in the P&S department.

Fill-or-Kill (FOK). An order that requires execution of the entire quantity immediately. If not, the order is cancelled.

Fiscal Year. The twelve-month period during which a business maintains its financial records. Since this cycle does not have to coincide with the calendar year, it is known as the fiscal year.

Flat. A bond trading without accrued interest is said to be trading "flat."

Floor Broker. An exchange member, who, as such, is permitted to conduct business on the exchange floor.

FOK. *See* Fill-or-Kill.

Free Stock. Loanable securities, that is, securities that can be used for loan for hypothecation. These securities are firm-owned shares or stock in a margin account that represents the debit balance.

Futures Contract. A long-term contract on an underlying instrument, such as a grain, precious metal, index, or interest rate instrument, by which the buyer and seller lock in a price for later delivery.

General Obligation (GO) Bond. A muni bond whose issuer's ability to pay back principal and interest is based only on its full taxing power.

GNMA. *See* Government National Mortgage Association.

GO. *See* General Obligation Bond.

Good-til-Cancelled (Open) Order (GTC). An order that does not expire at the end of the day it is entered. Instead, it remains in force until it is either executed or cancelled.

Government National Mortgage Association (GNMA). A government corporation that provides primary mortgages through bond issuances. Its securities are called Ginnie Maes.

Growth Stock. Stock of a company in a new industry or of a company participating in an emerging industry.

GTC. *See* Good-til-Cancelled (Open) Order.

Hypothecation. A brokerage firm's pledging of margin securities at a bank to secure the funds necessary to carry an account's debit balance.

Immediate-or-Cancel (IOC). An instruction on an order that requires as many lots as can be filled immediately and the rest cancelled.

Income Bonds. Bonds issued when the ability of the issuing company to pay interest is questioned. They are speculative instruments that pay high rates of interest.

Indenture. The terms of a corporate bond. Also known as deed of trust, it appears on the face of the bond certificate.

Industrial Revenue (ID Revenue, ID Revs, or Industrial Rev) Bond. A form of muni bond whose issuer's ability to pay interest and principal is based on revenue earned from an industrial complex.

Investment Banker. *See* Underwriter.

Issue. (1) The process by which a new security is brought to market. (2) Any security.

Legal Transfer. A type of transfer that requires legal documentation, in addition to the normal forms. Usually, in the name of a deceased person, a trust, or other third party.

Liability. Any claim against the corporation, including accounts payable, salaries payable, and bonds.

Limit Order. An order that sets the highest price the customer is willing to be paid or the lowest price acceptable. Buy orders may be executed at or below the limit price, but never higher. Sell orders may be executed at or above the limit price, but never lower.

Liquidation. (1) Closing out a position. (2) An action taken by the margin department when a client hasn't paid for a purchase.

Liquidity. The characteristic of a market that enables investors to buy and sell securities easily.

Listed Stock. Stock that has qualified for trading on an exchange.

Load. The sales charge on the purchase of the shares of some open-end mutual funds.

Loan Value. The amount of money, expressed as a percentage of market value, that the customer may borrow from the firm.

Long Position. (1) In a customer's account, securities that are either fully paid for (a cash account) or partially paid for (a margin account). (2) Any position on the firm's security records that has a debit balance.

Management Company. The group of individuals responsible for managing a mutual fund's portfolio.

Margin Account. An account in which the firm lends the customer money on purchases or securities on short sales. Customers must have enough equity in the account to pay for purchases by the fifth business day after trade or meet obligations that may be incurred immediately.

Margin Department. The operations department responsible for ensuring that customers' accounts are maintained in accordance with margin rules and regulations.

Market Maker. Another term for dealer or specialist. In the interest of maintaining orderly trading, a market maker stands ready to trade against the public and therefore to make a market in an issue.

Market Order. An order to be executed at the current market price. Buy market orders accept the current offer, and sell market orders accept the current bid.

Mark-to-Market. Process by which security position values are brought up to their current value. The customer may request the excess equity, or the firm may call for the deposit of additional funds. Either request is a "mark" to the market.

Maturity. The date on which a loan becomes due and payable—when bonds and other debt instruments must be repaid.

MCC. *See* Midwest Clearing Corporation.

Member. An individual who owns a membership (a seat) on an exchange.

Member Firm. A partnership or corporation that owns a membership on an exchange.

Merger. The combination of two or more companies into one through the exchange of stock.

Midwest Clearing Corporation (MCC). The clearing corporation of the Midwest Stock Exchange.

Minimum Maintenance. Established by the exchanges' margin rules, the level to which the equity in an account may fall before the client must deposit additional equity. It is expressed as a percentage relationship between debit balance and equity or between market value and equity.

Money Market Instruments. Short-term debt instruments (such as U.S. Treasury bills, commercial paper, and banker's acceptances) that reflect current interest rates and that, because of their short life, do not respond to interest rate changes as longer-term instruments do.

Mortgage Bond. A debt instrument issued by a corporation and secured by real estate owned by the corporation (such as factories or office buildings).

Muni. Slang for municipal bond.

Municipal Bond. A long-term debt instrument issued by a state or local government. It usually carries a fixed rate of interest, which is paid semiannually.

Municipal Note. A short-term debt instrument of a state or local government. Most popular are revenue, bond, and tax anticipation notes.

Mutual Fund. A pooling of many investors' money for specific investment purposes. The fund is managed by a management company, which is responsible for adhering to the purpose of the fund.

National Association of Security Dealers (NASD). A self-regulating authority whose jurisdiction includes the over-the-counter market.

National Association of Security Dealers Automated Quotation Service (NASDAQ). A communication network used to store and access quotations for qualified over-the-counter securities.

National Securities Clearing Corporation (NSCC). A major clearing corporation offering many services to the brokerage community, including comparison of NYSE, Amex, and over-the-counter transactions.

Negotiable. A feature of a security that enables the owner to transfer ownership or title. A non-negotiable instrument has no value.

Net Asset Value (NAV). The dollar value of an open-end fund divided by the number of outstanding fund shares. In an open-end fund quote, the NAV is the bid side; the other side is the sales charge.

New York Futures Exchange (NYFE). A commodities market located at 30 Broad Street, New York, New York, specializing in index futures.

New York Stock Exchange (NYSE). Located at 11 Wall Street, New York, New York, a primary market for buying and selling the securities of major corporations.

1933 Act. *See* Truth in Security Act.

1934 Act. *See* Securities and Exchange Act.

No-Loan Fund. An open-end fund that does not impose a sales charge on customers who buy their shares.

Not Held (NH). An indication on an order that the execution does not depend on time; the broker or trader should take whatever time is necessary to ensure a good execution.

OBO. *See* Order Book Official.

OCC. *See* Options Clearing Corporation.

Odd Lot. A quantity of securities that is smaller than the standard unit of trading.

Open-End Fund. A mutual fund that makes a continuous offering of its shares and stands ready to buy its shares upon surrender by the shareholders. The share value is determined by net asset value of the fund.

Option. A contract that entitles the buyer to buy (call) or sell (put) a predetermined quantity of an underlying security for a specific period of time at a preestablished price.

Options Clearing Corporation (OCC). A clearing corporation owned jointly by the exchanges dealing in listed options. OCC is the central or main clearing corporation for listed options. Options traded on any SEC regulated exchange can be settled through OCC.

Order Book Official (OBO). An employee of certain exchanges who executes limit orders on behalf of the membership.

Order Room. An operations department responsible for monitoring pending orders, recording executions, maintaining customers' GTC orders, and resolving uncompared trades.

Over-the-Counter Market. Comprised of a network of telephone and telecommunication systems over which unlisted securities and other issues trade. It is primarily a dealers' market.

P&S Department. *See* Purchase and Sale Department.

Pacific Clearing Corporation (PCC). The clearing corporation of the Pacific Stock Exchange.

Pacific Stock Exchange (PSE). This exchange operates in San Francisco and Los Angeles.

Par. Face value.

Par Value. A value that a corporation assigns to its security for bookkeeping purposes.

Participating Preferred. Preferred stock whose holders may "participate" with the common shareholders in any dividends paid over and above those normally paid to common and preferred stockholders.

Pass-Through Security. Instrument representing an interest in a pool of mortgages. Pass-throughs pay interest and principal on a monthly basis.

Penny Stocks. Extremely low-priced securities that trade over the counter.

Philadelphia Stock Exchange (PHLX). An equities and options exchange located in Philadelphia, Pennsylvania.

Point. A price movement of one full increment. For example, a stock rises one point when its price goes from 23 to 24.

Portfolio. The different securities owned in an account of a client. The more different securities are in the account, the larger the portfolio.

Pre-emptive Right. A right, sometimes required by the issuer's corporate charter, by which current owners must be given the opportunity to maintain their percentage ownership if additional shares of the same class are issued. Additional shares of the soon-to-be-issued security is offered to current owners in proportion to their holdings before the issue can be offered to others. Usually one right is issued for each outstanding share. The rights a predetermined cash amount are used to subscribe to the additional shares.

Preferred Stock. Stock that represents ownership in the issuing corporation and that has prior claim on dividends. In the case of bankruptcy, preferred stock has a claim on assets ahead of common stockholders. The expected dividend is part of the issue's description.

Preliminary Prospectus. *See* Red Herring.

Primary Market. (1) The initial offering of certain debt issues. (2) The main exchanges for equity trading.

Principal. A brokerage firm when it acts as a dealer and marks up a purchase price or marks down a sale price when reporting the execution.

Prospectus. A document that explains the terms of a new security offering—the officers, the outside public accounting firms, the legal opinion, and so on. Must be given to any customer who purchases new corporate and certain muni issues.

Proxy. A form and a process for voting via the mail, permitting stockholders to vote on key corporate issues without having to attend the actual meeting.

PSE. *See* Pacific Stock Exchange.

Public Offering Date. The first day the new issue is offered to the public, on or shortly after the effective date.

Purchase and Sale Department. The back office department responsible for figuration, comparing the trade, and issuing the confirmation.

Put. An option that permits the owner to sell a standard amount of an underlying security at a set price for a predetermined period.

Questionable Trade (QT). A form used when an NYSE-originated trade cannot be compared by the morning of trade date plus three.

Quote. The highest bid and lowest offer on a given security at a particular time.

RAN. *See* Revenue Anticipation Note.

Record Date. The day that an individual must be the owner of record to be entitled to an upcoming dividend.

Red Herring. The preliminary prospectus. The name comes from the advisory that is printed on the face of the prospectus in red ink.

Redemption. The retiring of a debt instrument by paying cash.

Refunding. The retiring of a debt instrument by issuing a new debt instrument.

Reg T Excess. In a margin account, the amount by which the loan value exceeds the debit balance.

Registered Form. The recording of a security's ownership on the issuer's central ledger. Anyone delivering the security must prove that he or she is, in fact, the person to whom the security is registered.

Registered Trader. A member of an exchange who is responsible for adding "liquidity" to the marketplace by purchasing or selling assigned securities from his or her inventory. Also known as competitive market makers or option principal members.

Registrar. A commercial bank or trust company that controls the issuance of securities.

Registration Statement. Document filed with the Securities and Exchange Commission (SEC) explaining an impending issue and pertinent data about the issuer. Based on the information provided, the SEC either permits or prevents the issue from being offered.

Regular Way Contract. The first contract sheet received from NSCC that contains compared, uncompared, and advisory data.

Regular Way Delivery. A type of settlement calling for delivery on the fifth business day after trade dates for stocks, corporate bonds, municipals. For government bonds and options, delivery is the first business day after trade.

Regulation T (Reg T). A federal regulation that governs the lending of money by brokerage firms to its customers.

Regulation U (Reg U). A federal regulation that governs the lending of money on securities by banks to their customers.

Rejected Option Trade Notice (ROTN). A procedure and form by which an uncompared listed option trade is returned to the broker who executed it for reconcilement.

Repurchase Agreement (Repo). An agreement used to finance certain government and money market inventory positions. The brokerage firm sells securities to the financing organization, with the agreement that the firm will repurchase them in the short-term future.

Restricted Account. As defined by Regulation T, a margin account in which the debit balance exceeds the loan value.

Revenue Anticipation Note (RAN). A short-term debt instrument that is issued by municipalities and that is to be paid off by future (anticipated) revenue.

Right. *See* Pre-emptive Right.

Round Lot. A standard trading unit. In common stocks, 100 shares make up a round lot. A round lot of bonds in the over-the-counter market is 5 bonds.

SCCP. *See* Stock Clearing Corporation of Philadelphia.

Secondary Market. The market in which securities are traded after the initial (or primary) offering. Gauged by the number of issues traded, the over-the-counter market is the largest secondary market.

Securities and Exchange Act (The 1934 Act). The Act governing the lending of money by brokerage firms (Reg T), including the short-sale (uptick) rule, and requirements regarding insiders or controlled persons.

Securities and Exchange Commission (SEC). The federal agency responsible for the enforcement of laws governing the securities industry.

Securities Industry Automated Corporation (SIAC). The computer facility and trade processing company for NYSE, Amex, NSCC, and PCC.

Segregation. The isolation of securities that the firm may not use for hypothecation or loan. The securities, which must be "locked up" by the firm, represent fully paid-for securities or the portion of a margin account in excess of loanable securities.

Serial Bonds. An issue of bonds that matures over a period of years.

Settlement Date. The day when a transaction is to be completed. On this day, the buyer is to pay and the seller is to deliver.

Settlement Date Inventory. The total of all positions in a security on settlement date, including vault, transfer, fails, and elsewhere.

Short Exempt. A phrase used to describe a short sale that is exempt from the short sale rules. For example, buying a convertible preferred, submitting conversion instructions, and selling the common stock before the stock is received.

Short Position. (1) A position in a customer's account in which the customer either owes the firm securities or has some other obligation to meet. (2) Any position on the firm's security records having a credit balance.

Short Sale. The sale of securities that are not owned or that are not intended for delivery. The short seller "borrows" the stock to make delivery with the intent to buy it back at a later date at a lower price.

SIAC. *See* Securities Industry Automated Corporation.

Size. The number of shares available in a quote. For example, if the quote and size on a stock is $9\frac{1}{4}-\frac{1}{2}$ 3x5, it means that the bid is $9\frac{1}{4}$, the offer is $9\frac{1}{2}$, 300 shares are bid, and 500 shares are offered.

Specialist. A member of certain SEC-regulated exchanges who *must* make a market in assigned securities. Specialists also act as two-dollar brokers in executing orders entrusted to them.

Spread. (1) A long and short option position in either puts or calls on the same underlying stock but in a different series. (2) The difference between the bid and offer sides of a quote. (3) In underwriting, the difference between what the issuer receives from the underwriter and what the underwriter sells the security for to the public on the offering.

Stock. A security that represents ownership in a corporation and that is issued in "shares."

Stock/Bond Power. A form used as a substitute for endorsement of a certificate. When completed and attached to the certificate, the security can be processed for delivery or transfer.

Stock Clearing Corporation of Philadelphia (SCCP). The clearing corporation of the Philadelphia Stock Exchange.

Stock Dividends. A dividend paid by corporations from retained earnings in the form of stock. The corporation declares the dividend as a percentage of shares outstanding.

Stock Loan Borrow. Part of the cashiering function, this operations department is responsible for lending excess seg stock and obtaining stock when needed by the firm.

Stock Record. A ledger on which all security movements and positions are recorded. The record is usually in two formats. One shows movements of the security the previous day and the other shows the current security positions.

Stock Splits. The exchange of existing shares of stock for more newly issued shares from the same corporation. Since the number of shares outstanding increases, the price per share goes down. Splits do not increase or decrease the capitalization of the company, just redistribute it over more shares. The effect is the adjustment to the trading price.

Stop Limit Order. This order is similar to a stop order, but it becomes a limit order instead of a market order. Buy stop limit orders are entered above the current market; sell stops are extended below it.

Stop Order. A memorandum order that becomes a market order when the price is reached or passed. Buy stops are entered above the current market price; sell stops are entered below it.

Straddle. Simultaneous long or short positions of puts and calls having the same underlying security and same series designation.

Street Name. A term of registration in which securities are registered in the name of a brokerage firm, bank, or depository; it is acceptable as good delivery.

Street Side. The opposing, or contra, firms' side of trades. For example, customer agency transactions consummated on an exchange must be offset and balanced against the "opposing firm" or street-side reports.

Strike (Exercise) Price. The price at which an option can be exercised. For example, the owner of a call ABC April 40 can call in (buy) 100 shares of ABC at 40; the strike price is 40.

Supplemental Contract. A contract issued by the clearing corporation that includes total of the regular way contract, adjustments made through advisories, and adds by seller processing.

Syndicate. The group that is formed to conduct an underwriting and that includes the underwriting manager and other underwriters.

Takeover. The acquisition of control over a corporation by another company, which normally ousts the current management. The takeover can occur by means of a proxy fight or the acquisition of a controlling quantity of common stock.

Tape. A broadcasting facility which disseminates listed trades in order of their occurrences.

Tax Anticipation Note (TAN). A municipal note issued in anticipation of revenues from a future tax.

Tax Exempt Bonds. Municipal securities (whose interest is free from federal income tax).

Tender Offer. The offer made by one company or individual for shares of another company. The offer may be in the form of cash or securities.

Trade Date. The day a trade occurs.

Trade Date Inventory. A term used by trading departments to mean the total of all positions of a security at the start of the trading day.

Trade-for-Trade Settlement. A form of settlement in which the buying clearing firm settles a trade directly with the selling firm. It excludes the use of any netting, CNS, or clearing system.

Transfer. The process by which securities are reregistered to new owners. The old securities are cancelled and new ones issued to the new registrants.

Transfer Agent. A commercial bank that retains the names and addresses of registered securities owners and that reregisters traded securities to the names of the new owners.

Truth in Security Act (1933 Act). A federal regulation governing the issuance of new corporate securities. This Act also covers certain municipal securities and mutual funds.

Two-Dollar Broker. An exchange member who executes orders from other member firms and charges a fee for each execution.

U.S. Treasury Bill (T Bill). The shortest-term instrument issued by the federal government. The maturities of these discounted issues do not exceed one year at issuance, with three-month (90-day) or six-month (180-day) paper being very common.

U.S. Treasury Bond (T Bond). The longest-term debt of the federal government, issued in coupon form for periods of 10 to 30 years.

U.S. Treasury Notes (T Notes). An intermediate debt instrument of the federal government, issued in coupon or interest rate form and usually for 1 to 10 years.

Underlying. (1) The security behind an option. (2) The commodity underlying a futures contract.

Underwriter (Investment Banker). In a municipal underwriting, a brokerage firm or bank that acts as a conduit by taking the new issue from the municipality and reselling it. In a corporate offering, the underwriter must be a brokerage firm.

Underwriting. The process by which investment bankers bring new issues to the market.

Underwriting Manager. (1) In a negotiated underwriting, the investment banker whose client is the corporation wanting to bring out a new issue. (2) In a competitive underwriting, the lead firm in a group that is competing with other group(s) for a new issue.

Uniform Practice Code. Part of the NASD rules that govern the dealing of firms with each other.

Unit. At issuance, a "package" of securities, such as a bond and warrant, which become separable at a later date.

Uptick. A listed equity trade at a price that is higher than that of the last sale.

Warrant. A security that allows the owner to purchase the issuing corporation's stock for a certain price over a stated period. That period could be 10 or 20 years, and the price of the conversion is much higher than the current price of stock issue. A warrant is usually issued with another security, such as one warranty plus one bond, both of which form one *unit.*

When Issued (WI). A phrase applied to securities that are about to be issued and whose settlement date is not set. Usually common stock issued under a rights offering trades "WI." Also, government bills auctioned on Tuesday but settled on Thursday trade in this manner.

Yield. The rate of return on an investment. There are as many computations as there are different yields, such as current yield and yield-to-maturity.

Index

A

Account executive, 80
Account maintenance,
  margin department, 145
Accounts
  types of, 81-85
    corporate accounts,
      84
    estate accounts, 85
    individual cash
      accounts, 81-82
    joint accounts, 83
    margin accounts, 83
    partnerships, 85
    pension accounts, 85
    power-of-attorney
      accounts, 84
    trust accounts, 85
Accrued interest, 102-6, 207
Added by seller, definition
  of, 207
Added trade contracts, 116,
  207
Administration
  American Stock
    Exchange (AMEX), 63

New York Stock
    Exchange (NYSE),
    53-54
ADR, *See* American
  depository receipt.
Advisory processing, 207
Agency transaction, 106,
  208
Agents
  brokers as, 9
  over-the-counter (OTC)
    market, 65-66
Allied members, 55-56
  New York Stock
    Exchange (NYSE), 55
All-or-none (AON) orders,
  95, 208
American depository receipt
  (ADR), 208
American Stock Exchange
  (AMEX), 8, 51-52, 59,
  63-64, 208
  administration of, 63
  AMEX Option System
    (AMOS), 96
  brokers, 64

membership
    requirements, 63
    Post Execution Reporting
        System (PERS), 96
Amex Option System
    (AMOS), 96
Asked, definition of, 208
Asked price, 72
As-of, definition of, 208
Assets section, balance
    sheet, 187-88
Assignment form, illustration
    of, 158
Auction, of U.S. Treasury
    securities, 42
Audit, 180-81

B

Bad delivery, stock
    certificates, 161
Balance sheet, 187-88, 208
    accepted formula for, 188
    assets section, 187-88
BAN, *See* Bond anticipation
    note.
Banker's acceptances
    (BAs), 39, 208
Bank-issued debt securities,
    39
Basis price, 209
Bearer bonds, 36
Bearer form, 209
Bearer instrument, 209
Beneficial owners, 163, 167,
    190, 193, 205-6, 209
    brokerage firms as, 202-6
Best efforts basis,
    underwriters acting on, 10
Bid, definition of, 62, 209
Bid price, 72
Big board, 209
Blotter, definition of, 209
Blue sky laws, 12
    definition of, 209
    state versus federal laws,
        12

Bond anticipation notes
    (BANs), 45, 210
Bond brokers, 60-61
Bond house, 68-69
Bond interest, 200
    accrued interest, 102-6
Bond power, 231
Bonds, 210
Book entry system, 42-43
Booking, purchase and
    sales department, 125
Book value, 210
Boston Stock Exchange
    (BSE), 52, 210
Bouncing delivery, 150-51,
    161
Box, 210
Break account, 178
Breakpoint, 210
Brokerage firms, 210
    as beneficial owners,
        202-6
    as stockholders of
        record, 197-200
    See also Member firms.
Broker-dealer firm, *See*
    Over-the-counter (OTC)
    securities house.
Brokers, 210
    American Stock
        Exchange (AMEX), 64
    at the market, 62
    definition of, 9
    difference between
        dealers and, 9-10
    exchanges, 52, 56-59
    New York Stock
        Exchange (NYSE),
        56-59
    commission house
        broker, 57
    registered floor trader,
        57
    specialists, 58-59
    two-dollar broker, 57
    over-the-counter (OTC)
        market, 65
Broker's broker, 69-70
Broker's call rate, 210

Broker-to-broker
comparison, 109
BSE, *See* Boston Stock
Exchange.
Business organization
forms of, 1-5
corporations, 4-5
partnerships, 3-4
proprietorships, 1-3
Buy-back, 165
Buying at the market, 92
Buying power, 132, 136-37,
211
Buy orders, 89
total/net amount, 126
Buy stop orders, 94

C

Callable, definition of, 211
Callable bonds, 37
Call (option), 47, 211
Capital gain, 211
Capitalization, 211
Capital loss, 211
Capital stock, 211
Cash accounting, 183-88,
211
closing the books, 186-88
credits/debits, 183-85
daily activity, 186-87
Cash accounts
definition of, 128
difference between
margin accounts and,
130-31
handling of, 128-30
rules governing, 129-30
Cash dividends, 190-91, 211
common stock, 15
dividend department,
190-91
Cashiers department,
149-72
functions of, 149-50
hypothecation (bank
loan), 164
receive/deliver, 150-62

clearing corporations,
155-57
continuous net
settlement (CNS)
system, 155-57
depository function,
152-54
good delivery, 157-61
institutional
customers, 155
money settlement, 158
settlement cycle,
150-52
settlement process,
161-62
reorganization, 171
security (stock) transfer,
165-72
steps involved in,
166-67
transfer section,
duties of, 167-70
transfer through
Depository Trust
Company (DTC),
170
spinoffs, 172
stock loans, 164-65
repurchase
agreements
(repos), 165
tender offers, 171-72
vaulting, 162-64
segregated (seg)
securities, 163-64
Cash sale, 211
CBOE, *See* Chicago Board
Option Exchange.
CBT, *See* Chicago Board of
Trade.
Certificates, 212
Certificates of common
stock, 16
Certificates of deposit
(CDs), 39, 212
CFTC, *See* Commodities
Future Trading
Commission.
Check the market, definition
of, 74

Chicago Board Option
    Exchange (CBOE), 8, 52,
    59, 112-14, 212
    Report Automated
        Execution System
        (RAES), 97
Chicago Board of Trade
    (CBT), 212
Chicago Mercantile
    Exchange, 212
Clearing corporations, 49,
    109-16, 212
    major houses, 115
    netting and, 151
    responsibility of, 115
    work of, 114-16
Clearing house comparison
    (CHC), 212
Close-outs, 147
Closing the books, cash
    accounting, 187-88
CME, See Chicago
    Mercantile Exchange.
CNS, See Continuous net
    settlement.
Collateral trust bonds, 38,
    213
Combination orders, 95
COMEX, 213
Commercial loans, 32
Commercial paper, 31, 213
Commission house broker,
    57, 213
Commissions, agency
    transactions, 103
Commodities Futures
    Trading Commission
    (CFTC), 11, 213
Commodity futures
    (commods), 52
Common stock, 213
    cash dividends, 15
    certificate of, 16
    definition of, 13
    dissolution, 15
    market value of, 17
    par value of, 17
    rights of common
        stockholders, 15
    stock dividends, 15

Compared trades, 112
Comparison, 213
    purchase and sales
        department, 101-26
    broker-to-broker
        comparison, 109
    clearing houses,
        109-16
    continuous net
        settlement, 118-19
    ex-clearing
        corporation trades,
        120
    how executed trades
        are compared, 109
    money settlement,
        119-20
    netted balance orders,
        116-18
Competitive option traders
    (COTs), 59
Confirmation, 213
Continuous net settlement
    (CNS), 118-19, 155-57,
    214
Contra broker, 108
Contract sheets, 110-12
Convertible bonds, 37, 214
Convertible debentures, 39
Convertible preferred stock,
    23
Cooling-off period, 214
Corporate accounts, 86
Corporate bonds, 31-39, 214
    definition of, 32
    face value, 32
    how bonds differ from
        stock, 35-36
    illustration of, 33
    interest rate, 34
    maturity date, 34
    purchase price, 34-35
Corporate resolution, 86
Corporations, 4-5
    advantages of, 4-5
    definition of, 4
    management of, 5
    and proxy department,
        205-6
    stockholders, 4

Coupon bonds
  types of, 36
    bearer bonds, 36
    callable bonds, 37
    convertible bonds, 37
    registered bonds, 36
    secured bonds, 37-38
    serial bonds, 36
    sinking funds, 37
    unsecured bonds, 39
Credit balance, 134-37, 214
Credit column, cash
  accounts, 128-29
Cumulative preferred,
  definition of, 214
Cumulative preferred
  dividends, preferred
  stock, 19, 22-23
Curb exchange, 214
Current market value,
  135-36
CUSIP, 110, 214
  definition of, 102
Custodial agreements, 86
Customer's account card,
  128
  credit column, 128-29
  debit column, 128-29
Customer's broker, 80
Customer's confirmation
  contents of, 122-25
  illustration of, 123

D

Daily activity, cash
  accounting, 186-87
Daily stock record, 177-79
Day order, 214
Day trade, 215
Dealers, 215
  dealer markup, 9
  definition, 9
  difference between
    brokers and, 9-10
  investment banking firms
    acting as, 10
  market makers, 9

over-the-counter (OTC)
  market, 65, 72
  as principals, 9
Dealer's broker, 69-70
Debenture bond, 215
Debentures, 39
Debit balance, 83, 128, 132,
  134, 215
Debit column, cash
  accounts, 128-29
Declaration date, 195
Deed of trust, *See*
  Indenture.
Delete of compared,
  definition of, 215
Deliver balance order, 116
Delivery
  bad delivery, 161
  bouncing delivery,
    150-51, 162
  good delivery, 147-48,
    157-60
  conditions for, 160
  physical delivery, 147,
    150
  of securities, 147-48
  See also Receive/deliver.
Deposit of margin, 138-39
Depositories, 197
  functions of, 152-55
Depository, 215
Depository Trust Company
  (DTC), 153, 162, 171, 215
Designated Order
  Turnaround (DOT)
  System, 97, 215
Director, 215
Dirty stock, 161
Discounted instruments, 45
Dissolution, 15
Dividend claim form, 198-99
Dividend department, 189-200
  cash dividends, 190-91
  claiming dividends for
    customers, 197-200
    accrued interest,
      102-6
  depositories, 197
  role of, 193-97
    declaration date, 195

dividend rate, 194-95
ex-dividend date,
    196-97
payable date, 195
record date, 195-96
stock dividends, 191
stock splits, 192-93
Dividend disbursing agent,
    190
Dividend rate, 194-95
Dividends, 215
    definition of, 23
    payment of, 23
    preferred stock
        cumulative preferred
            dividends, 19,
            22-23
        noncumulative
            preferred
            dividends, 19-23
DK, *See* Don't know.
DNI, *See* Do not increase.
DNR, *See* Do not reduce.
Dollar preferred stock
    dividends, 18
Do not increase (DNI), 216
Do not reduce (DNR), 216
Don't knows (DKs), 112,
    120-21, 150, 155, 216
DOT, *See* Designated order
    turnaround.
DTC, *See* Depository Trust
    Company.
Dually listed securities, 52
Due bills, 193, 216
Due date, bonds, 34

Excess equity, 135
Exchanges, 51-64
    American Stock
        Exchange (AMEX),
        63-64
    bond brokers, 60-61
    brokers, 52
        types of, 56-59
    commodity futures
        (commods), 52
    definition of, 52-53
    dually listed securities,
        52
    listing requirements,
        51-52
    members, 52-53
    New York Stock
        Exchange, 53-56,
        61-62
    odd lot transactions,
        59-60
    option exchanges, 52
    price fixing, 53
    regional exchanges, 52
    traders, 52
    See also American Stock
        Exchange (AMEX);
        Brokers; New York
        Stock Exchange
        (NYSE).
Exchange tickets, 124
Ex-clearing corporation
    trades, 120
Ex-dividend date, 190,
    196-97, 217
Exercise price, *See* Strike
    price.
Expiration month, 217
Extensions, 147

E

Effective date, 216
Equipment trust
    bonds/certificates, 38,
    216
Equity, 132, 133, 217
    excess equity, 135
Escrow receipt, 217
Estate accounts, 85
Excess, 135

F

Face value, 217
    corporate bonds, 32
Factor table, 217
Fail to deliver, 118, 151, 217
Fail to receive, 118, 217
Family of funds, 47

Fannie Maes, *See* Federal
National Mortgage
Association (FNMA).
Farmers Home
Administration (FmHA),
mortgages and, 43
Fast automatic stock
transfer (FAST), 217
Federal Home Loan
Mortgage Corporation
(FHMA) issues, 43
Federal Housing Authority
(FHA), mortgages and, 43
Federal laws, securities
industry regulations,
11-12
Federal National Mortgage
Association (FNMA)
issues, 43
Federal Reserve Board, 11
margin accounts and,
138-45
Regulation T, 127,
135-37, 142
Fed funds, 217
Figuration, 218
purchase and sales
department, 102-8
Fill-or-kill (FOK) orders, 95,
218
Finders, 165
Firm commitment basis,
underwriters acting on, 10
Firm quotes, 73
First preferred stock, 19
Fiscal year, 218
Flat position, 119, 218
Floor brokers, 54, 57, 108,
218
FOK, *See* Fill-or-kill orders.
Freddie Macs, *See* Federal
Home Loan Mortgage
Corporation (FHMA).
Free stock, 164, 218
Full power of attorney, 86
Futures contracts
buying and selling of, 48
definition of, 48, 218
going long, 48
going short, 48

terms/conditions of, 48

G

General obligation (GO)
bonds, 45, 218
Ginnie Maes, *See*
Government National
Mortgage Association
(GNMA).
GNMA, *See* Government
National Mortgage
Association (GNMA).
GO, *See* General obligation
bond.
Going long, 48
clearing houses and, 49
delivery of, 49
Going short, 48
Good delivery
conditions for, 160
stock certificates, 160-63
Good-til-cancelled (GTC)
orders, 191, 219
Government debt securities,
41-45
mortgage-backed
securities, 43-44
municipal bonds and
notes, 44-45
U.S. Treasury bills,
notes, and bonds,
41-43
Government National
Mortgage Association
(GNMA), 43, 219
Growth stock, 219
GTC, *See* Good-til-cancelled
(GTC) order.

H

Hypothecation agreement,
131-32, 219

I

Immediate-or-cancel (IOC)
   orders, 95, 219
Income bonds, 219
Indenture, 219
Individual cash accounts,
   83-84
   See also Cash accounts.
Industrial revenue (ID
   revenue, ID revs, or
   industrial rev) bonds, 219
Initial margin requirements,
   139-40
Inside quotes, over-the-
   counter (OTC) market, 72
Institutional Delivery Service
   (ID), 155
Interest expense, 149
Interest rate, corporate
   bonds, 34
Investment banking firms, 8,
   68
   acting on best efforts
      basis, 10
   acting as dealers, 10
   acting on firm
      commitment basis, 10
   See also Underwriter.
Issue, 219
Item-due messages, 146

J

Joint accounts, 85

L

Legal entity concept,
   corporations, 4
Legal transfer, 220
Lending agreement, 85
Liability, 220
Liability section, balance
   sheet, 188

Limited life, of partnerships,
   3-4
Limited power of attorney, 86
Limited price order, 58
Limited tax bonds, 45
Limit orders, 92-93, 96, 220
Liquidating an account, 129
Liquidating dividend, 24
Liquidation, 85, 220
Liquidity, 220
Listed securities, 220
   New York Stock
      Exchange (NYSE), 61
Load, 220
Loan value, 132, 135, 220
Long position, 220
Long sales, 89, 125
Lots, 59

M

Main stock record, *See*
   Weekly stock record.
Maintenance call, 138
Make a market, definition of,
   74
Management company, 220
Margin, time for deposit, 141
Margin accounts, 84-85,
   130-38, 220
   basic terms used in,
      132-38
      buying power, 132,
         136-37
      credit balance, 132,
         134-35
      current market value,
         132-37
      debit balance, 132,
         135
      equity, 132, 133
      loan value, 132, 135
      minimum maintenance
         requirements,
         137-38
      Reg T excess, 133,
         135-36

difference between cash
accounts and, 130-31
hypothecation
agreement, 131-32
regulation of, 138-40
initial margin
requirements,
139-40
minimum maintenance
requirements,
141-42
Regulation T, 139
restricted accounts,
140
special memorandum
accounts (SMAs),
141
time for deposit of
margin, 138
Margin calls, 140
Margin department, 127-48,
221
account maintenance,
145
case example, 141-45
handling cash accounts,
128-30
margin accounts
handling of, 130-32
regulation of, 137-41
responsibility of, 127
roles of, 145-48
account maintenance,
145
clearance for issuance
of checks, 146
close-outs, 147
delivery of securities,
147-48
extensions, 146
items due, 146
sales support, 145
Margin rate, *See* Initial
margin requirements.
Market makers, 9, 66, 71-75,
221
over-the-counter (OTC)
market, 71-75
asked price, 72
bid price, 72

Market orders, 92, 221
Mark-to-market, 221
Market value, common
stock, 17
Markup, 74
dealers, 9
principals' transactions,
104
Master file, customer, 84
Maturity, definition of, 221
Maturity date, corporate
bonds, 34
Maximum loan value, 137
MCC, *See* Midwest Clearing
Corporation.
Member, 221
Member firms, 8, 54, 221
trading in over-the-
counter (OTC)
markets, 10
Membership requirements
allied members, 55-56
American Stock
Exchange (AMEX), 63
New York Stock
Exchange (NYSE),
55-56
Merger, 221
Microfilming/microfiching of
documents, 82
Midwest Clearing
Corporation (MCC), 221
Midwest Stock Exchange
(MSE), 52
Minimum maintenance
requirements
definition of, 222
margin accounts, 139-40
New York Stock
Exchange (NYSE),
139-40
Money market instruments,
222
Money settlement, 119-20
Monthly cash entries, cash
accounting and, 186
Mortgage-backed securities,
43-44

Federal Home Loan
    Mortgage Corporation
    (FHMA) issues, 43
Federal National
    Mortgage Association
    (FNMA) issues, 43
Government National
    Mortgage Association
    (GNMA) issues, 43
Student Loan Association
    (SLA) issues, 43
trading of, 44
Mortgage bonds, 38, 222
Multiservice firms, 10-11
Municipal bonds, 44-45, 222
    kinds of, 45
    state/local notes, 45
    trading of, 44
Municipal debt securities,
    41-45
    mortgage-backed
        securities, 43-44
    municipal bonds and
        notes, 44-45
Municipal notes, 44-45, 222
Mutual funds, 47, 222

N

National Association of
    Securities Dealers
    Automated Quotation
    (NASDAQ), 75-76, 222
National Association of
    Securities Dealers
    (NASD), 70, 75, 222
    membership in, 70-71
National Quotation Bureau,
    76
National Securities Clearing
    Corporation (NSCC),
    115-16, 162, 223
Negotiable, 223
Net asset value (NAV), 223
Netted balance orders,
    11-13, 116-18
Netting, clearing
    corporations, 151

Net worth section, balance
    sheet, 188
New account form, 81
New York Curb
    Market/Exchange, 63
New York Futures Exchange
    (NYFE), 223
New York Stock Exchange
    (NYSE), 8, 51-52
    administration of, 53-54
    listing securities for
        trading on, 61
    membership in, 54-55
    membership
        requirements,
        55-56
    minimum maintenance
        requirements, 139-40
    trading on, 61-62
No-loan fund, 223
Nominee, definition of, 160
Noncumulative preferred
    dividends, 19-23
    preferred stock, 19-23
Nonparticipating preferred
    stock, 19, 22
No par value, 19
Notes, 31
Not held (NH), definition of,
    223

O

OBO, *See* Order book
    official.
OCC, *See* Options Clearing
    Corporation.
Odd lot transactions, 59-60,
    224
OKTP (OK to pay), 145
One cancels other (OCO)
    orders, 95
Open-end fund, 224
Operations, typical
    operations organization,
    79
Operations division, 77-86
    function of, 77-78

opening an account,
80-81
types of accounts, 81-85
corporate accounts,
85
estate accounts, 85
individual cash
accounts, 81-82
joint accounts, 83-84
margin accounts, 83
partnerships, 85
pension accounts, 85
power-of-attorney
accounts, 84
trust accounts, 85
Option contracts, 47-48
Options, 224
Options Clearing Corporation
(OCC), 224
Options exchanges, 52
Order book official (OBO), 9,
224
Order processing, 96-98
exchange system, 96-97
over-the-counter
executions, 97-98
Order room, 224
customers' orders, 87-89
order execution, 98-99
order form, 89-91
order match, 88
order processing, 96-97
short sales, 89, 95-97
types of order, 92-95
limit orders, 92-93, 96
market orders, 92
special-purpose
orders, 95
stop orders, 93-94, 96
Out of balance stock record,
178
Outstanding warrants, 29
Over-the-counter (OTC)
firms, 8
Over-the-counter (OTC)
markets, 65-76, 224
agents, 65-66
brokers/dealers, 67-68
dealers, 65, 72
market makers, 71-75

asked price, 72
bid price, 72
member firm trading in, 10
National Association of
Securities Dealers
(NASD), membership
in, 70-71
nature of, 65-67
over-the-counter firms,
68-70
bond house, 68-69
broker's broker, 69-70
dealer's broker, 69-70
investment banking
firms, 68
over-the-counter
securities house,
69
principals, 72, 108
publicizing OTC
quotations, 75-76
quotations in, 72-73
regulation of, 70
securities traded in, 67
trading in, 71, 74-75
Over-the-counter (OTC)
securities house, 69
Owner's liability,
proprietorships, 2

P

Pacific Clearing Corporation
(PCC), 224
Pacific Stock Exchange
(PSE), 52, 59, 225
Par, 225
Parent company, 172
Participating certificates
(PCs), 39
Participating preferred
stock, 19, 22, 225
Partnerships, 3-4, 84
definition of, 3
disadvantages of, 3
limited life of, 3-4
Par value, 17, 225

Pass-through certificates,
43, 225
Payable date, 195
Penny stocks, 225
Pension accounts, 86
Percent preferred stock
dividends, 18-19
Philadelphia Stock
Exchange (PHLX), 52,
59, 225
Pink sheets, 76
Point, 225
Portfolio, 225
Post, 61
New York Stock
Exchange (NYSE), 58
Post Execution Reporting
System (PERS), 97
Power-of-attorney accounts,
84
Power-of-attorney form, 84
Preemptive right, 225
"Preemptive rights" clause,
corporation charter, 25
Preferred stock, 14, 18-23,
226
definition of, 14, 18
dividends, 18-19
dollar preferred stock
dividends, 18
percent preferred
stock dividends,
18-19
no par value, 19
preferred stock
certificate, 20-21
types of, 19-23
convertible preferred
stock, 23
first preferred stock,
19
nonparticipating
preferred stock, 19,
22
participating preferred
stock, 19, 22
second preferred
stock, 19
Preliminary prospectus, See
Red herring.

Price fixing, exchanges, 53
Primary dealers, U.S.
Treasury securities, 42
Primary market, 226
Principals, 72, 226
dealers as, 9
over-the-counter (OTC)
market, 72, 108
Projection report, 162
Property dividend, 24
Proprietorships, 1-3
advantages of, 2
definition of, 1
disadvantages of, 2
owner's liability, 2
problem of raising capital,
3
Prospectus, 226
Proxy, 202-4, 226
Proxy department, 201-6
corporations and, 201-2
function of, 201
proxy, definition of, 202-4
record date, 204-5
stockholder vote by
proxy, 202
PSE, See Pacific Stock
Exchange.
Public offering date, 226
Purchase price, 62
Purchase and sales
department, 101-26, 226
booking, 125
comparison, 108-21
broker-to-broker
comparison, 109
clearing houses,
109-14
continuous net
settlement, 118-19
ex-clearing
corporation trades,
120
how executed trades
are compared, 109
money settlement,
119-20
netted balance orders,
116-17
customer's confirmation

amount, 124
commission, 124
preparation of, 122-25
SEC fee, 125
total/net amount, 125
figuration, 102-8
reconciliation, 120-21
recording, 102
tasks of, 101-2
Puts, 47, 226

Q

Quarterly cash entries, cash
accounting and, 186
Questionable trades (QTs),
112, 113, 227
Quotes, 66, 87, 227

R

Raising capital,
proprietorships, 3
See also Underwriting.
RAN, *See* Revenue
anticipation notes.
Receive/deliver, 150-62
clearing corporations,
155-57
continuous net
settlement (CNS)
system, 155-57
depository functions,
152-54
good delivery, 157-60
hypothecation (bank
loan), 164
institutional customers,
155
money settlement, 157
physical delivery, 150
reorganization, 171
repurchase agreements
(repos), 165
security (stock) transfer,
165-66

segregated (seg)
securities, 163-64
settlement cycle, 150-52
settlement process,
161-62
spinoffs, 171
stock loans, 164-65
tender offers, 171-72
vaulting, 162-64
Receive and deliver (needs)
report, 162
Reconciliation, purchase
and sales department,
120-21
Record date, 195-96, 227
proxy department, 204-5
Recording, purchase and
sales department, 102
Redemption, 227
Red herring, 227
Refunding, 227
Regional exchanges, 52
Registered bonds, 36
Registered floor trader, 57,
227
Registered representatives,
80
Registered securities, 148
Registrar, 227
duties of, 166-67
Registration statement, 228
Reg T excess, 131, 135-36,
227
Regular way contracts, 111,
116, 228
Regular way delivery, 228
Regulation
margin accounts, 137-41
initial margin
requirements, 137
minimum maintenance
requirements,
139-40
Regulation T, 137
restricted accounts,
140-41
special memorandum
accounts (SMAs),
141

time for deposit of
margin, 138-39
Regulation T (Reg T), 137,
228
Federal Reserve Board,
127, 135-37
margin accounts, 137
Regulation U (Reg U), 228
Rejected option trade
notices (ROTNs), 114,
228
Report Automated Execution
System (RAES), 97
Repurchase agreement
(repo), 228
Restricted accounts, 130,
140-41, 228
Revenue anticipation notes
(RANs), 45, 228
Revenue bonds, 45
Rights
common stockholders, 15
definition of, 24
issuance of, 25
rights certificate, 24, 28
stockholder exercise of,
25
value of, 24-25
See also Preemptive
rights.
Round lots, 59, 229
common stock, 13

S

Sale price, 62
Sales support, margin
department, 145
Sallie Maes, See Student
Loan Association (SLA).
SCCP, See Stock Clearing
Corporation of
Philadelphia.
Seat, New York Stock
Exchange (NYSE), 52
Secondary market, 229
See also Over-the-
counter (OTC) market.

Second preferred stock, 19
Secured bonds, 37-38
types of, 38
collateral trust bonds,
38
equipment trust
certificates, 38
mortgage bonds, 38
Securities and Exchange
Act (1934), 229
Securities and Exchange
Commission (SEC), 11,
229
regulations of, 11-12
Securities houses
types of, 7-8
investment banking
firms, 8
member firms, 8
over-the-counter
(OTC) firms, 8
Securities industry, 7-12
difference between
broker and dealer,
9-10
multiservice firms, 10-11
regulation of, 11-12
federal laws, 11-12
state laws, 12
securities houses,
types of, 7-8
underwriters, 10
Securities Industry
Automated Corporation
(SIAC), 229
Security transfer
cashiers department,
165-71
steps involved, 166-67
transfer section,
duties of, 167-70
transfer through
Depository Trust
Company (DTC),
171
Segregation, 229
Selected quotations,
National Association of
Securities Dealers, Inc.,
76

Sell orders, 89
  total/net amount, 125
Sell stop orders, 94
Semiannual cash entries,
  cash accounting and,
  186-87
Serial bonds, 36, 229
Settlement cycle, 150-52
  physical delivery, 150
Settlement date, 82, 104,
  230
Settlement date inventory,
  229
Shares, common stock, 13
Short exempt, 230
Short position, 230
Short sales, 89, 95-96, 130,
  230
SIAC, See Securities
  Industry Automated
  Corporation.
Signature, stock
  certificates, 160-61
Signature cards, 84
Sinking fund, 37
Size, definition of, 87, 230
Specialists, 71, 230
  New York Stock
    Exchange (NYSE),
    58-59
  functions of, 58
Special memorandum
  accounts (SMAs), 141
Special-purpose orders, 95
Spinoffs, cashiers
  department, 172
Spread, 58-59, 66, 72, 230
Spread orders, 95
State laws
  blue sky laws, 12
  securities industry
    regulations, 12
Stock, 13-30, 231
  dividends, 23-24
  rights and warrants,
    24-29
  certificate for, 29-30
  state versus federal laws,
    12
  types of, 13-14

common stock, 13,
  14-17
preferred stock, 14,
  18-23
Stock certificates
  bad delivery, 161
  good delivery, 157-70
  conditions for, 160
  signature, 160-61
Stock Clearing Corporation
  of Philadelphia (SCC),
  231
Stock dividends, 191, 231
  common stock, 15
Stock exchanges, See
  Exchanges; New York
  Stock Exchange (NYSE);
  American Stock
  Exchange (AMEX).
Stockholders, and
  management of
  corporations, 4-5
Stockholders of record,
  166-67, 189, 190, 193,
  197, 205
  brokerage firms as, 201-6
Stock loan borrow, 231
Stock loans
  cashiers department,
    164-65
  repurchase
    agreements
    (repos), 165
Stock power, 157, 159, 231
Stock record, 231
Stock record department,
  173-82
  audit, 180-81
  causes of errors, 181
  daily stock record,
    177-79
  how stock record is kept,
    174-77
  weekly stock record,
    179-80
Stock splits, 192-93, 231
Stop limit orders, 95, 231
Stop orders, 93-94, 96, 232
Straddle, 232
Straddle orders, 95

Street name, 160, 168, 193, 232
Street sale, 232
Strike (exercise) price, 232
Student Loan Association (SLA) issues, 43
Subject quotes, 73
Subscription rights, *See* Rights.
Supplemental contracts, 116, 232
Syndicates, 8, 232

T

Takeover, definition of, 232
Tape, definition of, 232
Tax anticipation notes (TANs), 45, 233
Tax exempt bonds, 233
T bills, 233
Ten-share round lot, 60
Tenants in common agreement, 84
Tender offer, 233
Tender offers, cashiers department, 171-72
Trade date, 82, 108, 233
Trade date inventory, 233
Trade-for-trade settlement, 233
Traders, 108
    exchanges, 52
    over-the-counter (OTC) market, 66
    See also Dealers; Market makers.
Trading floor, 61
Transfer, 233
Transfer agents, 166, 233
    instructions to, 168-69
Trust accounts, 85
Truth in Security Act (1933), 233
Two-dollar broker, 57, 233

U

Underlying, definition of, 234
Undermargined accounts, 140
Underwriters, 10, 234
    acting on best efforts basis, 10
    over-the-counter market, 68
    See also Investment banking firms.
Underwriting, definition of, 234
Underwriting manager, 234
Uniform Practice Code (UPC), 234
Unit, 234
Unlisted securities, trading of, 88-89, 96
Unsecured bonds, 39
Uptick, 234
U.S. Treasury securities, 41-43
    settlement of, 42-43
    T bills, 41-42
    T bonds, 41-42
    T notes, 41-42

V

Vaulting
    cashiers department, 162-64
    segregated (seg) securities, 163-64
Veterans Administration (VA), mortgages and, 43

W

Warrants, 234
    definition of, 25
    illustration of, 26-27
    issuance of, 29
    outstanding warrants, 29

warrant certificate, 29-30
Weekly cash entries, cash
    accounting and, 186
Weekly stock record, 179-80
When issued (WI), 234
Wholesale quotations, 76
Wire room, *See* Order room.
Work-out quotes, 73

Y

Yield, 234